Dear Reader,

I want to take the time to acknowledge the vital role of my sponsors.

Sponsors allow me the freedom to research and write about my perspective relating to living the Black expeience. Needless to say, big publishing houses require a degree of conformity, in which I have no interest.

As such, my sponsors have been the lifeblood of this work. Without them, I would be unable to deliever this message of social justice to my readership.

In an effort to materialize my appreciation, I ask all of my readers to visit the web-sites of the official sponsors listed below. Take advantage of the free services and salient content they have to offer. I hope they will enrich your persective, as they have mine.

Bello

www.thebaconandeggs.com
www.operatingwhileblack.com
www.smartaboutbusiness.com

DRIVING WHILE BLACK

THE MANIFESTO

Bey, Bello

Driving While Black: The Manifesto

A Few Things That Your Lawyer Wouldn't Care to Explain to You and a Bunch of Other Important Shit You Need to Know

Library of Congress Cataloging-in-Publication Data

ISBN-10: 0989476006

ISBN-13: 978-0-9894760-0-3

Printed in the United States of America

Book Design by (designer name)

Photos by (photographer name)

Editing by Precision Writing & Editing

First Edition: (May 2013)

10 9 8 7 6 5 4 3 2 1

DISCLAIMER

Congratulations, and welcome to your first step in Mastering the Human Technology of Driving While Black.

My name is Bello Bey, I will be acting as your coach for as long as you will have me. Please understand, I am your coach. *I am not your attorney*, and I do not provide legal advice. My job is to give you my perspective and administrative coaching. I provide the pieces and it's your job to put together the puzzle.

You have to take personal responsibility for your own educational process and actions. We all individually must take responsibility for our own interpretation, inferences and understanding of what we read and comprehend. I make no guarantees whether or not my opinions and explanations contained herewith apply in your particular situation. You're responsible for verifying any administrative coaching or process mentioned within the boundaries of this book and all associated content. It's your duty to be sure that what you choose to apply is proper for your situation. If you're uncertain of the lawfulness of what you intend to do:

You are to consult with an attorney of your choice before you do anything.

I suggest that you do not take anyone's word for fact (including mine) you must do your own research in order to make a competent and educated decision with anything you do in life.

Bello Bey

CONTENTS

ACKNOWLEDGEMENTS

I would like to express my deep gratitude to my wife and children; Zee, Deja, Myjah, and Brooklyn, for their patient, enthusiastic encouragement and useful critiques of my message throughout the writing process of this book.

I am particularly grateful for the tireless and personal assistance given to me by Roc and Gina.

I'd like to thank the following people for their contribution to this project:

C. Flowers, E. Dumas, J. Dubose, M. Fields, M. Steward, N. Turner, R. Fanning R. Abram, D. Anderson.

Special thanks should be given to my field research team for their guidance and valuable support and useful and constructive recommendations on this project.

J. Jinka, H. Tucker, K. Anderson

My special thanks is extended to my editor and writing coach Ava at PWE Writers.

Finally, I wish to thank my parents for their support and encouragement throughout my life's journey, thank you PawPaw and Sweety.

INTRODUCTION

According to historical records, more than 4 million *niggers* were freed from slavery in 1865. Since that moment in time, America has found many ways and many names by which they cleverly police former slaves and their families.

In the landmark case *Plessy v. Ferguson* (1896), Plessy, a Black man, was found guilty of violating a State law which required Blacks to use separate facilities than Whites in public. What is significant to me about this case is that Plessy was found guilty on the grounds that the law was reasonably exercised by the State's police powers based upon **custom, usage, and tradition**.

The *Plessy v. Ferguson* adjudication of "equal but separate" idea was eventually overturned in 1954 in the *Brown v. Board of Education* ruling. However, the *Plessy v. Ferguson* ruling stands as the hallmark of America's position on the complexities of race and social interaction and remains relevant in this modern day. It's evidence that the American culture at large agrees that White privilege is a cultural right extended to White people and obviously denied to Black people.

"It's the American way."

It's the essence of the customs, usage and the traditions of this country that has obligated me to write to you about each of us learning to develop our own individual, proactive and manageable strategy at the grassroots level, to deal with the deadly oppression that we face daily.

In this book, you will read about why and how "culture" is the key to unlocking the power needed to meet the challenges that come with being Black in America including the challenge of Driving While Black.

I will explain how and why *becoming* or being recognized as a White person in America implies special treatment. Why it's legitimized by this society that White people are inherently entitled to privileges not extended to Black people. In turn, we will also visit the reasons why being recognized as Black in most places in our world implies that we lack the education needed to be a virtuous, knowledgeable, and articulate person; one neither capable of engaging in public debate nor defending oneself in court.

You will read in this book why effectively rebutting the presumption that being Black makes you or I inadequate in some way is the most empowering skill you will develop in this modern day.

It is important for the reader to understand that as I write, I am conscious that the adjectives Black, Negro, Nigger, Minority and Colored may mean many things including, but not limited to, "property" (Dred Scott V. Stanford) but they are not words that describe members of the human race. When I use the noun "Black" in this book, I am referring to the people with increased melanin, who have tied their linage to ancient African. I use the term Black to exercise brevity.

BELLO BEY

CHAPTER 1 – BANKRUPT

"IN MY OWN COUNTRY FOR NEARLY A CENTURY
I HAVE BEEN NOTHING BUT A NIGGER."
- W.E.B. DUBOIS

Did you know that the United States of America is registered as a corporation and all of the law enforcement agencies are registered as well?

There is plenty of evidence including the federal law described as *Title USC 28 3002 (15) (A)* that lays claim to the fact.

And in this chapter, I will explain the significance of this fact and how it relates to the event of Driving While Black.

It's widely known that the people who operate corporations have a legal obligation to shareholders (local and foreign investors), and that obligation is to create profit. Corporations have no heart nor flesh to have feelings. Corporations put profit over people.

By law — corporations are morally bankrupt.

Racial profiling is a "business technique" that works very well when it comes to making money regardless of how it might make anyone feel.

It works like this; the fines, fees, liberties and seized property taken from The People, all increase the bottom-line for State (and private) agencies. And this helps to increase the salaries, bonuses, and the budgets of the people who operate these various law enforcement agencies and departments. It's like having a trained and armed collection agent confronting so-called debtors and requiring a payment from them, whether they owe or not.

Because this business technique is so profitable, you and I would be foolish to believe that the people who use racial profiling in the line of duty as corporate agents will let up on using this profitable technique for no good business reason.

To understand why this racial profiling technique works so well, we have to dig into human nature a little bit. We will go into culture first.

The **dominant culture** in America is not that of the indigenous or native culture, but is that of the conqueror who is sometimes called "European" or White. It's customary for the conqueror of a body of land to establish for that territory institutions of education, institutions of law, political institutions, etc. All of which are used to teach the conqueror's language, values, rituals, artistic express, system of law and customs to all of the people occupying that land. Throughout history the victor of war writes the history books and they also write the laws. I presume that they are written to be read, but many people choose to skip the reading and proceed in pursuing life with little direction.

In America, minorities are known to assimilate to the dominant culture while occasionally participating in their families' subculture. For many people this is a simple life choice that requires little discussion or debate. Many people join the dominant culture and use that culture as catalyst in creating relationships and building "bonds" with others in an effort to forward their own interest and raise their families' quality of life.

This four letter word "bond" plays a major role in regard to the racial profiling technique that is being used today. The word bond simply means promise. What it suggests when used in the context of "building bonds between people" is that one or more person(s) is making a promise to treat another with honor, respect, consideration and vice versa. People use culture to build these bonds, which is why people have social gatherings with food and entertainment.

And because there's politics associated with America's dominant culture, social classes are created and recognized when people interact with each other in a cultural context. A person's class status is largely defined by the type of education s/he represents.

The 28th President of the United States – President Woodrow Wilson – is quoted as saying, at time when so many important decisions were made about how we live today:

"We want one class of persons to have a liberal education, and we want another class of persons, a very much larger class of necessity in every society, to forgo the privilege of a liberal education and fit themselves to perform specific difficult manual tasks."

- Woodrow Wilson

This suggests that America's leaders have (since the abolishment of slavery) intended to establish a working-class, by teaching people to be just that, "workers".

By definition a working-class is a laboring class that is primarily paid a below average income.

The trouble is that America made a "promise" to The People that we all would enjoy and be treated with equality.

But, many people do not feel as if the government intends to keep that promise.

Today, hidden or placed out of reach from the working-class is the key to our freedom and dignity... We are kept from the type of education that would allow us the ability navigate efficiently in real-world conditions and in situations where the best solution isn't well-defined.

The Harvard College of Admission, on their website explains this hidden type of education as thus:

The Value of a "Liberal Arts" Education

A Harvard education is a liberal education — that is, an education conducted in a spirit of free inquiry undertaken without concern for topical relevance or vocational utility. This kind of learning is not only one of the enrichments of existence; it's one of the achievements of civilization. It heightens students' awareness of the human and natural worlds they inhabit. It makes them more reflective about their beliefs and choices, more self-conscious and critical of their presuppositions and motivations, more creative in their problem-solving, more perceptive of the world around them, and more able to inform themselves about the issues that arise in their lives, personally, professionally, and socially. College is an opportunity to learn and reflect in an environment free from most of the constraints on time and energy that operate in the rest of life.

A liberal education is also a preparation for the rest of life. The subjects that undergraduates study and, as importantly, the skills and habits of mind they acquire in the process, shape the lives they will lead after they leave the academy. Some of our students will go on to become academics; many will become physicians, lawyers, and businesspeople. All of them will be citizens, whether of the United States or another country, and as such will be helping to make decisions that may affect the lives of others. All of them will engage with forces of change — cultural, religious, political, demographic, technological, planetary. All of them will have to assess empirical claims, interpret cultural expressions, and confront ethical dilemmas in their personal and professional lives. A liberal education gives students the tools to face these challenges in an informed and thoughtful way.
~ The Task Force on General Education

It's implied and understood that if one does not have such of an education such as the education provide by an Ivy League school similar to Harvard then s/he is less likely to effectively communicate a notable position in public debate (like a traffic stop) or defend his or her self in court as one might need to do in the aftermath of a traffic stop.

So, the question becomes who has this type of education and who doesn't.

The fast answer to this question is; anybody who wants this type of an education can have it.

But we all know that is *BULLSHIT!*

Here's why; truancy laws compel parents to enroll their children in the public school system as a toddler. From that point forward their education process is controlled by State-issued programs and curricula. The trouble is not what the public school curricula are teaching but rather what it doesn't teach. That being the case, the child must find another source to find a more applicable life skill building curricula. But chances are that the adults in that child's life are pre-occupied with their own lives of busy work, either searching for steady income, or being faced with the endless cycle of re-training requirements imposed on the working class in the globalized market place. Beyond that, most working class people don't know what a liberal or liberal arts education is or its value.

So, either by design (like President Woodrow proposed), or by misfortune for the American former slave families and working-class folks, the "elites" receive an elite (liberal) education and vocational skills are shoved at everyone else.

How does this relate to racial profiling?

The elite social class in America's dominant culture is synonymous with European, White man, conqueror, white privilege, white supremacy. Which is a concept, theory, ideology and business model that is primarily forwarded for the purpose of economic exploitation and much less for the purpose of exercising some blood thirst or xenophobic agenda.

Nevertheless, the techniques that are encouraged by the prejudiced policies appear at face value as acts of war on Black people for the sake of cruelty and brutality, although the primary strategy may be based in economic exploitation.

Without doing much evaluation in the area of race, the American society at large presumes that a White motorist or someone who might pass as White is entitled to the benefits of White privilege automatically.

Alternatively, the American society at large presumes that a Black motorist:

1. Is not entitled to the same courtesies as those extended to Whites by way of cultural heritage;

2. Has a mere vocational education at best, which implies that they make a low income and have little knowledge or resources needed to engage in public debate nor defend themselves in a court of law.

In this White culture, Black skin implies that we lack the benefits of a liberal education which has the effect of making us socially irresponsible, unable to be analytical in judgment and unable to take advantage of economic opportunities. Anyone who is suffering from symptoms such as these mention above are easily beatable in the game of claims and contracts that we all play every day. When we individually experience this type of defeat, we grow frustrated with our status in society.

It's a lie to suggest that being stereotyped and mistreated is somehow our fault. But it happens so often that we begin to question our own cultural ways as if we can behave in a way (culturally) that can reverse that presumption made by others that Black people are hopeless, helpless and inadequate unless proven otherwise on an account by account basis.

Like I said — this place is morally bankrupt.

To combat the position that society has taken against us, we (Black people) should look to the dominant culture for an example of what we could do to be more enculturated rather than simply attempting to assimilate. Those who may pass for White may be able to assimilate totally and reap the benefits of that but Black people can never totally assimilate, only partially. Which leaves us wanting for much more, and that is not equality. The difference between the two is that to enculturate means to adapt, and assimilate means to "become" or to make similar.

Black people cannot become White in this society because Black people are the definition of "different" than White people; therefore, we cannot be similar no matter how much we may try.

But what we can do is recognize that in the American mainstream culture, litigation is how the economic game is played. The court room is always the backdrop for the dealings between each other. In this litigious society, the only way to be considered worthy of respect (other than White privilege) is to have the ability to engage in serious negotiations, public debate and if all fails, the ability to be a threat in the event that a lawsuit(s) is found necessary.

Black people must enculturate, and refrain from attempting to assimilate because White supremacy and privilege are a large part of the American culture and Black people aren't entitled to White privilege.

We must adapt.

In this book we will dive deep into adapting by using the strategy and techniques needed to rebut the unforgivable presumption that we aren'thing less than prepared and capable of managing our own affairs, legal or otherwise.

However, in the next chapter, we will review some hard facts and numbers that will remind us what we are up against and why we need to become better at protecting ourselves when interacting with others as a Black men and women in this world.

CHAPTER 2 – THE WAR ON BLACK PEOPLE

RADICAL SIMPLY MEANS GRASPING THINGS AT
THE ROOT. - ANGELA DAVIS

WHAT IS THE WAR ON DRUGS?

The war on drugs is largely administered through local and state police officers by furthering traffic stops and escalating traffic stops to search for illegal drugs such as marijuana. This although statistics suggest an estimated fatality rate for marijuana related use was fewer than 4,000 while tobacco and alcohol took close to 400,000 lives in the same year.

There is no mechanism more damaging than a "Terry Stop" to minorities in America because of intimidating institutional procedures practiced by local, state, and federal level agents of our government. The War on Drugs only adds to the abuse of power used by these agents, which leads undereducated minorities to consent to unwarranted financial and criminal obligations out of fear and deceitful tactics.

The term "War on Drugs" was given birth to in 1971 when President Richard Nixon and his administration pulled it out of their asses. The so-called initiative includes a set of drug policies of the United States that is claimed to discourage the production, distribution, and consumption of illegal psychoactive drugs. The puzzling part of the actions of those involved in this "War of Drugs" is that we are hard pressed to find a more concentrated and longer standing drag net of enforcement focus as we do this initiative's focus on the Black and Latino communities.

Year to date, it's the 41st anniversary of this initiative and its devastating effects on minority motorists. There is no evidence that the War on Drugs has been effective in anything other than continuing America's racist legacy. Better said — there is no evidence that the war on drugs is not code for "The War on People of Color".

Drug peddling and drug use aren't just restricted to ethnic and racial minorities in the United States. Believe it or not, the numbers of White folk that use drugs far outnumber minorities — five times as many Caucasians are drug users as minorities. However, the war on drugs has, since time immemorial, been targeted at men and women of color. The unavoidable result of this process is the fact that skin color is now a proxy for criminality — ugh!

This opinion has created the profile that has resulted in more stops of minorities — especially Black motorists. As mentioned earlier, this premise is FACTUALLY erroneous.

According to US government reports, 80% of the nation's cocaine users are Caucasian, and the typical cocaine user is a "middle-class, Caucasian suburbanite."

Law enforcement agents employ tactics that focus on the inner city drug trade. Naturally, the jails and prisons are packed with minority drug law offenders, thus feeding the misconception that a large number of drug dealers and users were

Black and Latino.

With the emergence of the crack market in the 1980s, the color of one's skin became the chief profile component. To a large extent, Black travelers in the country's airports find themselves the subject of indecent searches and frequent interrogations by the US Customs and DEA Service.

Yes, it can be very annoying to have to endure an invasive body search — just because you're Black does not mean that you have cocaine shoved up your butt!

Most times, the sheer discriminatory nature of "profile" stops and searches were so obvious that judges actually took notice.

WHAT ARE THE FACTS

On the night of November 24th, 2006, two young men, both 23 years of age, were arrested in Los Angeles. The men were returning from two different parties on this Friday night when they were stopped in a traffic violation.

Mark D. failed a sobriety test. He also fought with the police officers when they tried to stop him from getting back in his car. He was arrested and taken to the station where he was searched. The search turned up 45 grams of cocaine in a plastic bag. Mark was booked that night but released in the morning. He was charged with a DUI (his second within a year) and told to appear before a judge within a month. Mark was also able to escape a possession conviction but was ordered into drug rehabilitation and community service. Mark is a White man.

James A. was stopped for a traffic violation. One of his rear lights was off. Police officers frisked him and searched his car. They found 6 grams of crack in his car. James was booked that night and remained in jail until his hearing. The public defender appeared on his behalf and James was told that since he had more than 5 grams of crack in his possession, he would serve the minimum penalty which is 5 years in prison. James is a Black man.

For over 30 years, Black Americans have seen racial profiling and discrimination become a stark reality in their daily lives. The 'War on Drugs' epitomizes the complex American history that spans social, political, economic, and criminal justice factors.

But if someone thinks that the war on drugs using Black America as its target began in the 1980s, they would be very much mistaken. Black youth have been used as vectors for the lucrative drug business since the 1960s. Many Black historians believe that the drug business was pushed into communities not only to disband them but to trap youth in the criminal justice system and limit their opportunities to leave impoverished areas behind.

Some researchers go further on this subject like Melanin theorist Carol Barnes who writes in his book Melanin: The Chemical Key to Black Greatness that white scientists deliberately created drugs such as, but not limited to, cocaine so these highly addictive drugs would be better structured to bind chemically with melanin. Barnes claims that because of this chemical engineering that Black people would likely get addicted faster and stay addicted longer.

America's war on drugs has gone hand in hand with the oppression of minority groups. Opium was tied in the early 1900s to Chinese immigrants while marijuana was tied to Mexican Americans in the 1930s. Crack was again tied to the Black community in the 1980s as part of an expansion of the war on drugs declared a decade earlier. In every instance, pursuing drug searches, arrests, and convictions were and continue to be about exerting social control over minority communities.

Human Rights Watch released a report in 2009 that looked at drug arrests and convictions based on FBI records. Their report tracked these numbers from 1980 to 2007:

- In every year from 1980 to 2007, Blacks were arrested across the country on drug charges at rates 2.8 to 5.5 times higher than White arrest rates.

- From state-by-state data from 2006, Blacks were arrested for drug offenses at rates in individual states that were from 2 to 11 times greater than the rate for Whites.

In every year between 1980 and 2007, arrests for drug possession arrests made up 2 out of every 3 drug arrests. In the period from 1999 through 2007, 4 out of every 5 drug arrests were for possession.

But, are Black men and women more likely to be drug users? Is that why they are disproportionately represented in drug-related arrests, convictions, and incarcerations?

The figures indicate that Black men and women are OVER-REPRESENTED in these drug-related criminal justice actions due to racial discrimination.

According to the Kennedy School of Government, the figures are as follows:

Percent of drug users who are Black: 15%

Percent of drug arrestees who are Black: 37%

Percent of drug convictions who are Black: 59%

Percent of drug incarcerations who are Black: 74%

The United States Supreme Court recommended to Congress that a **safety valve** be expanded to include all drug offenders in Criminal History Category II.

This safety valve would mean that those convicted of drug offenses carrying mandatory minimums would be eligible for relief from these mandatory minimums.

In 2010, thousands of people convicted of a drug offense with a mandatory minimum were relieved of the penalty through the safety valve. However, to continue the deep racial bias of the War on Drugs and the criminal justice system, Blacks benefited far less than others:

Black defendants relieved of minimum penalty: 9.8%

White defendants relieved of minimum penalty: 26.9%

Hispanic defendants relieved of minimum penalty: 36.8%

Other races relieved of minimum penalty: 29.5%

WHAT IS THE (SAD) TRUTH?

The sad truth is that Black men and women pay a very high price for this country's drug policy. It's really a social policy disguised as a drug one; a social policy designed to create a racial caste system to undo the gains of the civil rights movement.

When a Black man or woman is convicted of a drug offense, they are labeled a 'felon' in the long-term. Their experiences with educational institutions, health care facilities, employers, welfare and child welfare offices, lawyers, police, and courts are mostly negative. The felon designation puts these men and women in the role of a 'criminal'.

People in prison cannot vote in 48 states. In some states, people on probation and parole are also denied the right to vote. In 11 states, people are denied the right to vote after they have finished serving their sentences.

Given that about 1 in 7 Black men is disenfranchised in some way through the judicial system, the rights of millions of Black men to participate in voting and the exercise of their democratic rights are taken away.

Every arrest, conviction, and incarceration of a Black man or woman on a drug charge leave a cascade of negative effects. These affect the person, his or her family, and the community. It's possible to quantify the long-ranging devastation of Black communities by the War on Drugs without considering the following:

- **Reduced employment**

More than 60% of employers surveyed in Los Angeles said they would not hire a person with a criminal record. Between 1999 and 2004, the number of criminal background checks has doubled. One out of every five background checks is performed on a Black man or woman with a criminal record.

Beside the massive industry built on background checks, Blacks with a criminal conviction are much more likely to be denied employment. Virtually shut out of any meritorious and paid position but the lowest, most predatory ones arranged by the state.

It's not unusual, then, that many of these men and women will return to prison within 5 years. The system is set up so that they are forever marginalized and excluded from legal economic system.

Reduced income leads directly to lost income and impoverishment in the short-term and the long-term. The consequences of this are a lifetime of financial struggles and a high likelihood of working under the table and being forced to deal with predatory lending institutions.

- **Family separation impact on children**

Over 2.6 million children have a parent in prison. According to the US Department of Justice, 1 in 15 Black children has a parent in prison. In comparison, 1 in 42 Hispanic children and 1 in 111 White children have a parent in prison.

Having a parent in prison is very hard on children. They are much more likely to live and grow up in poverty. They are also more likely to be withdrawn, have fears of abandonment, and perform poorly in school.

Children of incarcerated parents are also more likely to become disruptive in school, suffer bullying, and drop out altogether. The effects on their lives and their futures are tremendous. And they are generational. When these children find themselves being taught in decrepit schools in poor areas, targeted by police, and shut out of the social and economic mainstream, they are at higher risk of being caught in illegal activities and becoming prisoners themselves.

- **Housing barriers and instability**

Every year, about 700,000 people are released from prison. About 1/3 are homeless before or after imprisonment.

People with a conviction on their records can be denied housing. Not only does it make it difficult to reintegrate the person from prison, it may lead to exploitation with high rent rates and punitive fees.

To make things worse, public housing, which is an affordable alternative, can be denied to these individuals housing access.

- **Debt and impaired credit ratings**

Drug convictions and incarcerations are devastating for the Black community in high debts and poor credit ratings. According to the Justice Department, when an incarcerated person is released, they face a mountain of debts.

A lot of the debt is accumulated child support payments while the incarcerated parent has no income. The individual also faces lots of expenses levied by the correction system in the form of surcharges, fines, and fees. It's not unusual for a person to be released and find themselves owing $10,000 or more in expenses.

In many counties and states, inmates are responsible for the costs of DNA and other evidentiary assessments to prove their innocent. These expenses are waiting for them when they are finally released.

These obligations waiting for the released individual can be insurmountable. Especially since the individual is unlikely to have any assets or ready employment upon release. The consequence is that the person is chased by several departments from child welfare to corrections, looking for payment and petitioning for wage garnishes.

- **Physical and mental health problems**

More than half (53%) of people in prison suffer from substance abuse and/or dependence. Of these individuals; about 17% receive treatment for their substance abuse problem in prison. Black men and women released from prison suffer from a number of physical and mental health problems. These problems, such as Post-traumatic Stress Disorder, can lead to depression, anxiety, and other symptoms.

Physical illnesses are also rampant such as high blood pressure and diabetes. Those released from prison are much less likely to find employment and have health insurance. This means that they are less likely to have primary health care for their physical and mental health problems.

1986 - WHAT HAPPENED?

The DEA introduced an annoying, racially biased courier profile to the highway patrol in 1986. Translation: DWB is not a new thing, it has been going on since the time Black people could afford to drive and own vehicles!

WHAT IS THE GOVERNMENT DOING?

When Nixon announced that drug use was "public enemy number one," he and his administration started a set of criminal justice policies that presidents following him continued. Before this early 1970s announcement, drug abuse was considered by policy-makers to be a social problem that should be treated. When dealing with users (who now make up 80% of those arrested), those early policies followed the medical model of treatment.

Nixon changed all that and so did policy-makers. The war on drugs didn't care much for the medical model and became a law enforcement issue which needed to be dealt with through aggressive, and many times pre-emptive, criminal justice policies.

In 1973, the government and policy-makers called for more strict penalties for drug possession, use, and sales. This lead to the creation of statutes known as the Rockefeller Drug Laws. These laws meant that people caught with drugs could face mandatory minimum sentences of fifteen years to life for possession of four ounces of narcotics.

These laws were enacted in New York first. Then they became model laws adopted by other states. Before the end of the 1970s, they also became the model for the country's national drug control policy.

Within this same year (1973), Nixon created the Drug Enforcement Agency (DEA) within the Department of Justice. The DEA was designed to become the federal government's lead agency for controlling drugs in the United States.

It's not a surprise, then, the criminalization of drug use make the prison population in the United States skyrocket. The war on drugs fed and grew the prison system while it enlarged the drug enforcement system simultaneously. Since minorities were especially targeted for this war, it's not surprise that they made the majority of prisoners incarcerated on drug charges.

The war on drugs gained traction and new energy under Reagan in the 1980s. The alarms were sounded over crack cocaine and its prevalence poor and Black communities. This was especially the case when promising, All-American college basketball forward Leonard ('Len') Bias died of a cocaine overdose at 22 in 1986. Headlines fueled the moral outrage over drug use in Black communities.

This national outrage led to the Sentencing Reform Act of 1984. This Act lead to Reagan administration creating the United States Sentencing Commission that developed the federal sentencing guidelines. It also led to the creation of the Anti-Drug Abuse Act of 1986, which poured millions of dollars in fighting the drug war and building new prisons. The bill also leads to the furtherance of mandatory minimum penalties for drug offenses.

These minimum penalties, however, like nearly everything about the US's criminal justice system came to embody the racial discrimination inherent to the system.

Drugs consumed by Black addicts were punished FAR more severely than similar ones consumed by White addicts.

With its sentencing, the judicial system created a difference in minimum penalties between Black people and White people that is 100-1. This sentencing disparity exists for the possession or sale of crack (used mostly by Black people) in comparison to cocaine (used mostly by White people).

What does this disparity mean in practical sentencing terms?

An individual who is caught with 5 grams of crack would receive the same five-year sentence in federal prison as individuals caught with 500 grams (or half a kilo) of powder cocaine.

Since Black addicts were the majority of crack users and White addicts were the majority of powder cocaine users, it was only a matter of time when Black users filled all the new prisons being built. And White addicts? They escaped minimum prison sentences, for the most part, and managed to escape all the consequences of becoming felons.

No sense can be made of this disparity other than it's richly and deeply entrenched in racial discrimination. Powder cocaine is no less addictive or harmful or more likely to cause violent behavior than crack. Any justification for the sentencing disparities failed to address these simple facts.

The Reagan administration wasn't done with its criminalization of drug use. In 1988, it passed the Anti-Drug Abuse Act of 1988. This law created the Office of National Drug Control Policy. This policy, along with the 1986 one, has shaped the drug laws that policy-makers follow to this day.

The War on Drugs is a war on Black people. For more than half a century, it's been an effective way to decimate Black communities, push Black people out of the formal economy, and profit from the imprisonment of young Black men and women. This War has achieved everything it has set out to achieve.

Learning to defend ourselves from America's prejudiced policies is our own responsibility because the stakes are too high to leave this responsibility to another person who may or may not have an ulterior motive.

CHAPTER 3 - STONEWALLING LIKE ALWAYS

THE THING WORSE THAN REBELLION IS THE
THING THAT CAUSES REBELLION.
- FREDERICK DOUGLASS, RECONSTRUCTION

WHAT IS STONEWALLING?

The State of Mississippi officially ratified into law the 13th Amendment of the U.S. Constitution of on February 7, 2013 (Google it).

The 13th Amendment was adopted by the U.S. In 1865 which had the effect of abolishing slavery.

Mississippi's State government representatives claim that they made a mistake, an oversight, accident or there was a glitch that went uncorrected for about 150 years.

This also means that slavery was legal in the state of Mississippi up until this "oversight" was fixed (Feb. 7, 2013).

Maybe that's why the prisons in Mississippi looked so much like plantations being worked by slaves.

I call this a transparent act of "Stonewalling" which allowed the Jim Crow mentality to carry on in the State of Mississippi for far too long.

Definition;

stonewall |'stōn, wôl|

verb [trans.]

delay or block (a request, process, or person) by refusing to answer questions or by giving evasive replies, esp. in politics : *the highest level of bureaucracy stonewalled us* | [as n.] (**stonewalling**) *the art of stonewalling and political intimidation.*

Stonewalling is a common practice used by people to exercise illegitimate powers. Stonewalling can in some cases be deadly to an unsuspecting person. It's the act of stonewalling that has replaced the German Shepherd Hounds and the powerful fire department operated water hoses previously used against Black people during the Civil Rights movement. Stonewalling has replaced the effect that segregated restrooms, water fountains and cafes across the nation once had on us mentally.

When people choose not to cooperate with what is right and just for a reason that cannot be articulated by that person, that is the act of stonewalling.

Growing up in Seattle Washington, it was rare for someone to deny me a right by claiming that because of my skin or ethnicity, I was not entitled, but very often I was delayed or diverted away from my right by the act of stonewalling. The person or people stonewalling would reserve plausible deniability by simply not stating a claim (or lying) for their lack of cooperation but refusing to cooperate with me all the same.

I am careful when it comes to generalizing but in this case I am willing to say that every single law enforcement agent and agency has learned or will learn the act of stonewalling as a strategy to exercise illegitimate power over the People in attempts to govern.

Any and every time a law enforcement agent asks you for your license and registration without entertaining or refusing to answer your questions, is that act of stonewalling.

Preparing yourself to defuse the effects of stonewalling is your job.

WHAT IS DRIVING WHILE BLACK?

It was 5:30 on a Monday morning and, like most people who work at the post office, Reginald (not his real name) drove the 10 miles to the sorting facility in relatively light traffic. No sooner did the 51-year old make a right turn into the main road than a police vehicle began tailing him very closely. He was going at the speed limit and didn't think much of it. After a mile or so, the officer lit his lights and Reginald parked by the side of the road. The officer seemed to take a full five minutes to come to Reginald's window and tell him that he made a rolling stop. Reginald was sure that he didn't because he never rolled at stops. A professional driver with the post office for more than 26 years, he just knew he didn't. But this wasn't the first time that he was stopped, mostly in light traffic, when no one was around.

Reginald's story is not much different than Jasmine's* (not her real name). The 22-year old worked the midnight shift at the local pharmacy. She was stopped one evening by a police officer. Like the one who stopped Reginald, this police officer called for backup, and only when the second cruiser arrive did Jasmine get someone to talk to her. The female officer who approached her asked for her license and registration, both of which were fine. Then the officer told her that she didn't signal to change lanes. Jasmine was also shocked when the officer told her that she will be arrested for outstanding traffic tickets. At that moment, she understood why the backup police vehicle showed up.

All of this happened to Jasmine right by the main road to her place of work. She was distraught as she stood by the side of the road, her hands cuffed behind her back. She didn't even have a cell phone on her to call her boss. When she was put in the back of the police vehicle, the tears started rolling down her face. *Why? Why?* She kept thinking to herself. Two police cars, her hands in cuffs, her car impounded. *All for what?* She wasn't a criminal. She didn't do anything. They didn't even write a ticket for the alleged illegal lane change. What does that mean? If she did make it, why didn't they give her a ticket for it? The only thing she could think of was that it was an excuse to stop her.

These are two stories of millions of stories. Black men and women of all ages, all professions, all social and economic classes. They have one THING in common. They drive while black.

Driving While Black is a rewording of the traffic charge for intoxicated driving. It refers to police officers stopping, questioning, ticketing, and even searching the cars of Black motorists. More often than not, these drivers haven't committed any crimes and a traffic ticket is used an excuse to stop them.

The financial, physical, and emotional impact of targeted traffic stops on Black men and women is very high. As Jasmine will recall, she felt so much humiliation and anger when arrested. To this day, she feels stress when she sees a police vehicle. Reginald will also tell you about learning to not take it personally but that it always stays under the surface. The knowledge that he was stopped for no other reason than that he is a Black man.

Young Black men and women will talk about their parents telling them to just SUR-VIVE a traffic stop. Don't talk back. Keep your hands within the officer's sights. Don't raise your voice. In fact, don't say anything at all, if you can. That's what Reginald tells his two college-aged sons. "Don't let them get to you". "Just get through it and go about your way".

WHAT ARE THE FACTS

The Bureau of Justice Statistics says that a traffic stop is the most common reason for a citizen to come in contact with the police. What else do the statistics say?

In 2008, Black drivers were about three times as likely as White drivers and about two times as likely as Hispanic drivers to be searched during a traffic stop. They also say that surveyed Black drivers were more likely to say that their stops and searches aren't justified.

Black drivers fare much worse after a stop than White or Hispanic drivers. Black drivers are twice more likely to be arrested than White drivers (4.5% vs. 2.1%). Hispanic drivers are arrested in 3.1% of traffic stops. Black drivers also receive worse, more brutal treatment. When stopped, Black drivers nearly 3 times more likely to be subjected to the police's use of force and/or the threat of force than White drivers. Black drivers are also 2 times more likely to be subjected to this force than Hispanic drivers.

What kind of force is used against Black drivers in a traffic stop? Black drivers report verbal abuse, the use of pepper spray, striking, kicking, grabbing, and forcefully being put on the ground.

The experiences of Black drivers that they are stopped just for being Black are supported by research done over a two decade period. In his chapter in the book, 'Race, Ethnicity, and Policing: New and Essential Readings', David A. Harris documented this research. Newer data has since been added by civil and human rights groups.

- In New Jersey over a 10-year period to the late 1990s, 73.2% of those arrested in a traffic stop were Black when Black motorists were only 13.7% of those on the road. The numbers reflected cars with either a Black driver and/or Black passenger.

- In Maryland, a research study of over 6,000 cars in 1994, over 72% of drivers stopped and searched were Black. This is despite official numbers showing that Black drivers committed only 17.5% of traffic violations on the road. So this means that Black drivers' traffic violations that necessitate a stop were very close to their percentage of the population. So why do they make up 3 out of 4 traffic stops and searches?

- In Ohio, court files from traffic stops during the 1990s that resulted in arrests showed that Black drivers are twice as likely to be issued traffic tickets as White drivers. These figures did not include stops that did NOT include arrests.

- In West Virginia, a February 2009 study of traffic stops and searches showed that Black drivers were 1.6 times more likely to be stopped than White drivers. Hispanics were 1.48 times more likely to be stopped than White drivers. With each traffic stop, Black and Hispanic drivers were almost twice as likely to be arrested. This is the case even when White drivers are more likely to be in the possession of illegal substances than non-White drivers.

- In Minnesota, a large study that examined data from across the state in 2002 found that Black, Hispanic, and Native American drivers were stopped and searched in a traffic stop than White drivers. Black drivers were more than twice as likely to be stopped as White drivers. Just like in West Virginia, White drivers were more likely to possess illegal substances than non-White drivers. The study put some figures down for what would happen if racial profiling was NOT part of traffic stops. If all drivers were stopped at the same rate in the 65 jurisdictions in the state, then:

  - 22,500 more White drivers would have been stopped,
  - 18,800 fewer Black drivers would have been stopped, and
  - 5,800 fewer Hispanic drivers would have been stopped.

- In Illinois, the state passed an Illinois Traffic Stops Statistics Act in 2003. Data that was collected after the passage of the Act showed that Black drivers and Hispanic drivers were twice as likely to be searched after a traffic stop. When the data of the searches considered as "consented were analyzed for the presence of illegal substances, White drivers were more likely to have illegal substances in their cars than Black and Hispanic drivers. Just as statistics show in Minnesota and West Virginia.

- In Texas, a research study in 2005 found that Black and Hispanic drivers were much more likely to be stopped and searched than White drivers. In some cases, Black drivers were three times as likely to be stopped as White drivers. Even though law enforcement authorities were more likely to find contraband on Whites. And just like in Illinois, West Virginia, and Minnesota, White drivers were more likely to have illegal substances in their cars than Black and Hispanic drivers.

- In New York, the New York Police Department collected data from 2005 to the middle of 2008. The results showed the following:

  - Approximately 80% of total traffic stops made were of Black and Hispanic drivers, who make up 25% and 28% of New York City's total population, respectively. In this same data period, only about 10% of traffic stops were of White drivers, who make up 44% of the city.
  - White drivers made up 8% and Black drivers made up 85% of all those frisked by the NYPD, in general. Also, 34% of White drivers stopped during this period were frisked while 50% of Blacks and Hispanic drivers stopped were frisked.
  - In this period, 17% of White drivers, compared to 24% percent of Black and Hispanic drivers had physical force used against them during NYPD-initiated encounters. This pattern of physical force use is shown in other states.
  - When the number of stops made during the three and one-half year period is added, just 2.6% resulted in the discovery of a weapon or contraband. Even though weapons and contraband yield were very small across all racial groups, stops made of White drivers proved to be slightly more likely to yield contra-

band. This is supported by evidence in other states that White drivers are more likely to possess illegal substances in their cars than Black and Hispanic Drivers.

- In Los Angeles, the Los Angeles Police Department collected traffic stop figures from July 2003 to June 2004. When these figures accounted for violent and property crime rates in specific LAPD reporting districts, they showed that:

  - Per 10,000 residents, the Black driver stop rate was 3,400 stops higher than the White driver stop rate.
  - Black drivers were 76% more likely to be stopped than White drivers. Hispanic drivers were 16% more likely to be searched than White drivers.
  - Black drivers were 127% more likely to be frisked than White drivers while Hispanic drivers were 43% more likely to be frisked than White drivers.
  - When Black drivers were stopped, they were 29% more likely than White drivers to be arrested. Hispanic drivers were 32% more likely than White drivers to be arrested.
  - Black drivers who consented to searches were 37% less likely to possess weapons, 23.7% less likely to possess drugs, and 25.4% less likely to possess any other type of contraband than consensual searches of White drivers. This is the same case as the other states covered above.
  - Hispanic drivers who consented to searches were 32.8% less likely to possess weapons, 34.3% less likely to possess drugs, and 12.3% percent less likely to possess any other type of contraband than consensual searches of White drivers.

- In Arizona, data collected in a two year period of 2006-2007, highway patrol officers stopped Black drivers at a rate of 2.5 times of White and Hispanic drivers. These officers also stopped Native American drivers at a rate of 3.5 times of White drivers.

WHAT IS THE (SAD) TRUTH?

The sad reality is that Driving While Black is a living, on-the-ground expression of racial profiling. It's not only young, Black males who are stopped, arrested, and threatened on American roads, although they probably fare much worse than others. Black drivers of all ages and economic conditions are subject to stops and searches. Just for being Black. Wealthy celebrities and inner-city teenagers alike.

The full impact cannot be quantified. Car seizures, bail money, lawyers' fees, missed work, records, and more. All of these add up to a levy on Black drivers, a racial profiling tax. This is not to add the mental, emotional, and spiritual effects that linger in the Black man and woman's minds.

But when Black drivers explain what traffic stops mean to them, they are met with blank stares or 'playing the victim' charges. The numbers don't lie. But Black men and women are expected to take it and not complain. Even when all the fingers point to two indisputable facts:

- Black drivers are NO MORE likely to commit traffic code violations than White or other ethnic drivers, and
- White drivers are MORE likely to possess illegal substances in their cars than Black drivers.

Both of these facts blow big holes in the theory that stopping, searching, and arresting Black drivers are all justified based on traffic violations and their likelihood of carrying illicit substances.

WHAT IS THE GOVERNMENT DOING?

For decades, the Supreme Court allowed police departments to stop and search cars without a warrant if they suspect the presence of illegal substances or evidence of a crime. They called this a '**Pretextual**' traffic stop.

In 1996, the Supreme Court made a direct comment on the constitutional legality of these types of stops in *Whren v. United States*. The Court rules that police can use traffic stops to investigate their suspicions of illegal substance possession or crime commission. And that police can have this right even if enforcement of the traffic code is not part of the stopping and/or searching of the driver.

The Supreme Court basically gave the greatest latitude for police departments to use traffic stops for non-traffic enforcement purposes. When White drivers, who aren't as affected by these stops, as Black drivers are citing the Fourth Amendment, they use the "catching criminals" arguments.

The data, however, shows that racial profiling changes this purpose dramatically. Black drivers who have committed no crimes are much more likely to be stopped, searched, and arrested. And White drivers who may have illegal substances in their cars are LESS likely to be arrested because of this racial targeting.

- Black drivers bear the brunt of this Supreme Court decision to give police departments full reign of using traffic stops as pretexts for non-traffic law enforcement. In a clear pattern of racial profiling and targeting, Black drivers continue to be stopped, frisked, searched, and arrested more than White drivers. Even though White drivers across a number of states show time and time again that they carry more illegal substances and contraband.

But the Supreme Court claims that racial profiling violates the constitutional requirement that all persons be accorded equal protection of the law in its Whren v. United States. According to the "Guidance Regarding the Use of Race by Federal Law Enforcement Agencies" that was issued by the U.S. Department of Justice in 2003:

- "Racial profiling" at its core concerns the invidious use of race or ethnicity as a criterion in conducting stops, searches and other law enforcement investigative procedures. It's premised on the erroneous assumption that any particular individual of one race or ethnicity is more likely to engage in misconduct than any particular individual of another race or ethnicity.

- Racial profiling in law enforcement is not merely wrong, but also ineffective. Race-based assumptions in law enforcement perpetuate negative racial stereotypes that are harmful to our rich and diverse democracy, and materially impair our efforts to maintain a fair and just society.

So if racial profiling is "wrong", "ineffective", and "perpetuates negative racial stereotypes", **why is it common across the country?**

With all the evidence that shows that Black drivers do not commit more traffic code violations OR possess illegal substances and contraband, **why are they still targeted for traffic stops?**

When White drivers are more likely to have illegal substances and contraband in their cars, **why are they frisked and searched LESS often than Black and Hispanic drivers?**

The only answer that makes sense is that racial discrimination is a systematic and endemic phenomenon in how the government deals with Black men and women. It seems that Black men and women behind the wheel need special protection from the police.

Who should we ally ourselves with for protection?

Who should Chavis Carter have turned to for help?

Protection which was needed for Chavis Carter. The 21-year old Black man was a passenger in a truck pulled over by police in Jonesboro, Arkansas on July 28, 2012. The young man died from a gunshot wound to the head while in police custody that night

What happened is a closely hidden mystery. According to the police, he possessed a gun which he used to commit suicide following his arrest. They've allegedly arrested him for having a small bag (10grams) of marijuana after being searched.

The mystery that caused the outrage was that, despite being frisked two times by the police's own admission, Carter managed to hide a gun which he used to shoot himself in the head. With his hands cuffed behind his back.

According to the autopsy report, "he was cuffed and placed into a police car, where apparently he produced a weapon, and despite being handcuffed, shot himself in the head."

Regardless of what happens in the Chavis Carter's case, Black men and women are all too aware of What Driving While Black means in their lives (or deaths).

With this chapter, I wanted you to be as surprised (or not) as I was when researching Driving While Black. It's a real stark injustice and systematic legal victimization of Black men and women.

In the next chapter, we will talk about how it feels to be pulled over by an over reaching law enforcement agent.

BELLO BEY

CHAPTER 4 – BUSINESS AS USUAL

IF YOU DON'T LIKE SOMETHING, CHANGE IT. IF
YOU CAN'T CHANGE IT, CHANGE YOUR ATTI-
TUDE. DON'T COMPLAIN.
- MAYA ANGELOU

When you see the police car lights flashing in your rear-view mirror or your side mirrors, your first instinct is to turn down the volume of your car radio and hope that the police aren't coming to get you.

Then, all your wishing vanishes as soon as you hear the 'Whuuurp, wuurp, wurp' sound.

It feels like your whole body reacts to the noise and lights; you go through a sort of trauma:

FIRST	Your heart skips a beat (or two).
SECOND	Your throat stops working for a split second as it drops.
THIRD	You begin to feel a subtle flutter of the butterflies in your stomach.
FOURTH	Without thinking, you lip a few curse words
FIFTH	You feel a sudden burn or sting in your chest, neck, and head cavity.
SIXTH	Different thoughts go through your mind in a flash about what you should do or say.

And all this stuff happens within a matter of a few seconds.

Why?

When I get pulled over even today, my mind and body goes haywire. I actually have to gather my breathing and find the focus to switch my mind and methods to dealing with this Driving While Black event.

It's ALWAYS a major event for me.

If you or I know that all of our legal stuff is in order, then this process is less intense - right?

But, you still go through anxiety because of the uncertainty about who, *what, when, and how* this so-called routine stop will go down.

Now, on the other hand, if you know that your driving license is expired, you have an outstanding warrant, you're suspended, intoxicated, violating some court order or you got "work" (meaning you have something that the law enforcement officer will mistake as contraband), then you may feel like dropping dead right on the spot from the pressure of facing the situation. I have personally been in this situation too many times.

A "Terry Stop" is what most law enforcement agents call a traffic stop, in reference to the landmark case Terry v. Ohio.

MY HIGH SCHOOL YEARS

1992 - I was about sixteen years old, driving a 1977 Monte Carlo; it was like an old tank (in a bad way). In my passenger seat was Kevin, and Norman was in the back seat, e-40's "I'm Going Federal" was playing in the CD player. Kevin and Norman were teammates on my high school football team, Rainier Beach High.

Around three o'clock on a Friday afternoon, we were making our way down Rainier Avenue in Seattle Washington headed downtown to Memorial Stadium where we were scheduled to play against another high school around 6 p.m. that evening.

About an hour prior to this, all of the players and coaches met in our high school locker room for Chalk Talk and to get our uniforms on as we usually did.

I noticed in the rear-view that this police car was sharking me from a few cars back. Soon enough, he started passing cars recklessly and I assumed he was coming after me. I had not seen him prior but he must have seen me somewhere a few blocks back.

As I suspected it would, the squad car began to follow us for a few miles.

When I got to Genesee Blvd., which was a major intersection, I took advantage of cars merging and accelerated and broke away from the squad car before he put on his lights to pull me over.

I pulled my car in to a Safeway grocery store parking lot hoping that they weren't actually following me as I suspected and I could let them pass.

My main concern was that I didn't have current insurance on the vehicle that was required by State statue at that time, and I did not want to get pulled over and face being fined the $475.00 for no insurance.

Most people can relate to the fact that it's expensive for young people to maintain a car and the associated expenses, especially when your family is barely making ends meet at home. Police are more than aware of these circumstances and they expect us to be deficient in some way.

In high school, I had insurance off and on for years because sometimes I would forget to pay the (expensive) policy or sometimes I used the money for something else like clothes or shoes. I was a teenager and I acted like it in regard to my responsibilities sometimes.

Back to the story. So, as I pulled into the parking lot, the police car passed me by. I smiled in relief. I recall having butterflies and my heart was pounding in my eardrums as I made the risky move to speed off and park before they could get close enough to signal me to pull over.

My friends could tell that I was nervous so we finally broke the silence in the car for the last mile or so, all laughing about me over reacting. I parked the car in a parking spot to gather myself for a moment while my friends poked fun at me a little. Just then, I looked in my mirror and the police car had doubled back and blocked my car in with the lights on and the siren on silent.

These dudes were playing a game of cat and mouse with me.

Over the loud speaker, one of them says, "Driver, turn the car off and drop the keys out of the window". Now my nervousness has instantly returned and now it has grown to anger because this surely isn't a normal traffic stop. I had not done anything to be stopped and, definitely, nothing to merit this type of treatment.

The officer says, "Driver step out of the car and place your hands on the roof of the car." Now, mind you, they are still inside their police car with their doors closed, and I cannot see in their car because of the glare on the windshield of their car.

I do as told. Then, one by one, he has my friends do the same. Next, the officers exited their car with their guns drawn and they, too, were both Black (I was glad to see this).

They approached us and proceeded to pat each of us down. I found this to be ridiculous because we had on our football pants full of pads and not pockets. My friends said nothing and just stared at the floor passively. I asked what this is about and one of the officers told me to shut up.

At that point while keeping my hands on the car, I began to argue, shouting curse words at these two violators. Apparently, between my rapid-fire expletives, I managed to raise some issues or questions that put them on their heels and I could see it in their faces. I told them that they had no right to stop me in the parking lot of Safeway because it's private property and they didn't offer any rebuttal to my claim.

Because I was so irate, I managed to gain the attention of a group of union workers who happened to be on a picket line in front of the store. The union workers began to gather around the altercation between the police and me.

This made the officers visibly uncomfortable. I could read that in the eye contact they were making with each other. I could tell they knew that this was getting out of control and they needed to make a move to end it. So one of them tells my friends to get their stuff and walk because they were taking me to jail for talking shit. This just made me talk more shit.

They handcuffed me for all to see and put me in the back seat of their squad car. One of them wrote me a ticket for defective equipment (I had a crack in my windshield) and a ticket for "NO PROOF OF INSURANCE" (dammit, that ticket is $475.00 every time). After I signed the tickets, they turned me loose. I picked my friends up and we made it to the game on time. This is when you (the readers) say, "That's BULLSHIT!"

Why did that have to happen? Do you know? I would say it happened because I was racially profiled and treated as a gang member before they ever asked me any questions. They were still trained to be Boys in Blue, even though they were Black like me.

MY COLLEGE YEARS

The highway to the college I attended was a rural and boring five-hour drive from my dorm room tower to the front door of my parents' house. In my first semester in college, I was unable to play football because of my SAT scores. I never did test very well. I think that test was something like 5 hours long including the breaks. Getting me to focus on something for 5 hours as a teenager? Yeah, right.

Anyway, the college I attended had a population of approximately 24,000 people including staff members and only 437 of them were considered Black. I was not comfortable hanging out at school any more than I had to.

Keg parties and frat functions aren't how I liked to kick it.

So my roommate and I drove home to Seattle on Fridays and back to school (in my 1994 hatchback Honda Accord) 15 out of the 18 weekends in the semester.

One of the small towns that we had to drive through to get back in forth from school is called Colfax, Washington.

In Colfax, the speed limit was something like 20 or 25 miles per hour, no kidding.

It was rumored that Colfax Washington was the last place in America to hold a legal lynching, and this place smelled of White Supremacy and former slave owners. Needless to say, fortunately, we survived the many runs through Colfax without being put in a tree like *Strange Fruit* - as Billie Holiday would say.

Being young and foolish, my friends and I, on the road from school, were always trying to beat the speed traps and set new records of making the 5 hour drive shorter and shorter.

Those small town governments were intent on catching ALL speeders, because that's how they feed their local economies.

In the really long stretches of the highway, they actually had Aircraft Monitoring, which they used to track speeds by timing how fast a vehicle traveled between quarter mile markers that they had painted on the shoulder of the highways. The aircraft (crop plan) would be up so high you may never see hit but, like magic, a highway patrol unit would be waiting to direct you to stop and "take your ticket", like it was a flyer to a party.

Using this system, they could pull over groups at a time with one unit. I must have given those towns in Kittitas County close to five thousand dollars in fees and fines over a two-year period.

That was more than 15 years ago but I would bet that this business model is still thriving for those small towns in Washington. One thing I will acknowledge about all this speeding and policing in between my home and college is that I was only asked for permission to search my car one time in those many encounters, which I declined and was immediately returned to my liberties. They were focused on writing ticket(s) and getting back to the Trap (speed trap that is).

MY ADULT YEARS

In my adult life, I experience far less contact with law enforcement in general. I believe this is because of my preference to being invisible in plain sight. Because of my experience with discrimination, and my experience with economic street and Black markets, I aimed to be aware of my surroundings.

I learned that it's far better to be clever than aggressive in this American culture.

I abandoned my youthful need for speed and recklessness behind the wheel. I took responsibility for having all of the proper licenses, insurance bonds, registrations, and anything else that I thought would save me from some unwanted ordeal.

As a young adult, my taste for finer automobiles drove me to keep an expensive European car.

Driving more attention grabbing cars actually had a reverse effect on being pulled over. I assume that the police didn't bother with me because I appeared to have money, which made me more capable to defend myself civilly.

I did actually use that perception in my favor when keeping nice tasteful things in plain sight but nothing that gave a whisper of a Black culture. I travel with expensive sunglasses, luggage, business books, financial books, and audio-tapes.

To me, this gave the appearance that I am capable of taking some action to protect myself legally, if I felt abused in anyway. I was careful to look and act the part of a person who might have the financial and intellectual means to raise and pursue a civil rights issue if they created one.

Because I had been pulled over a handful of times, and treated with respect and courtesy, and given warnings for breaches of some kind, I could smell the bad intention of an officer who was working outside of his capacity as a public servant when conducting a normal traffic stop. Like when a cop asked me to step out of the car.

This is a huge red flag.

Two words come to mind... Rodney - King!

It just seems unsafe (for everybody) for me to step out of the car to talk.

"We are talking just fine like we are" is what I say.

I think all Black people will agree that the phrase: "Step out of the car so we can talk" is almost always a lie. Or maybe not an outright lie but at least a half-truth. The translation is: "Step out of the car so I can slap the bracelets on you or trick you into doing something so I can warrant a search of your car without your consent".

As an adult, I found it ridiculous that I would feel so helpless when the police would jump behind me for no apparent reason and pull me over. Or they would watch me drive by traveling in opposite directions and they would flip a U-turn and race to catch me but only when they have seen the color of my skin. Frustrated and concerned, I began to do some research.

I looked for how others were dealing with being abused when they were Driving While Black, and I found many Black people complaining out of frustration about their encounters but not many with solutions or any idea of a productive way to deal with it.

HOW CAN I GET BETTER AT THIS DWB THING - I ASKED MYSELF

Because of my experience, I have chosen to dissect the business of being Black and master the event of Driving While Black. In doing so, I have found some best practices in various writings that we should all know and possibly use on a daily basis.

So I compiled and summarized what I gathered into a process that I will share with you which was born out of a combination of study and life's experience.

What I intended to do is help you protect yourself and your property against foolishness or unlawfulness. It's not intended to help do harm or especially to commit any violent act.

Those types of things will do none of us any good and would only lead to worse conditions for us collectively.

What you'll read from me will help you (especially if you're Black) to prepare for financial and legal obstacles such as participating in a so called "Terry Stop".

You will gain a better understanding of how to assert yourself while maintaining your own social and moral values. Ultimately, I hope to help you achieve your own style of self-preservation and wealth building ways.

No matter how small and petty, or how huge and ridiculously extravagant, your desired goals are, you can reach them with the right principles and processes.

More than just defusing the effects of Driving While Black, hopefully what you will read here will help you manage your daily dealings with others more productively. I submit to you that you can prepare for the business of being Black more efficiently if you take the time to develop a strategy and invest in your own education with radiance.

If you have made it to this part of the book, then I am willing to bet that you're the type of person who is a high achiever and who takes full responsibility for the results you get in life and business.

I hope that I can motivate you to keep going in life and business no matter your setbacks.

It took courage to pick up a book with such a politically incorrect title, and even more courage to actually read it. It's that same intellectual courage that will better prepare us for the event of *Living* While Black in the future.

In the next few chapters, my goal is to show you that your story (and/or mine) is woven into a greater fabric of deception and predation.

That the Black experience is somehow designed to tie each and every one of us in a private struggle of survival and defensive positioning but to hide that it's the larger, public policy behind it all.

CHAPTER 5 - WHO REPRESENTS

YOU LEARN ABOUT EQUALITY IN HISTORY AND
CIVICS, BUT YOU FIND OUT LIFE IS NOT REALLY
LIKE THAT. - ARTHUR ASHE

As long as we have God given sovereignty over our own affairs, and we govern ourselves in a first class way by refraining from delimiting the rights of others, then you
and I have the authority to exercise our rights and our constitutional "protections"
all the way - and every day.

To assert ones rights as a Black person can be a formidable task - there's no doubt
about that.

The people who have been elected to operate America's government have done or
allowed to be done everything necessary to criminalize Black men and their families, consequently often when we challenge another person, we are made to be the

villain rather than the victim (almost automatically) in the minds of most Americans.

Or we are accused of playing the race card, as if there is some "unfair" advantage gained by questioning whether race is an issue when conflict arises.

Let's just accept it, we (Black people) are deemed as violent and disparaging criminals in the subconscious minds of the average American. This is just our reality; there is no need to continuously judge it, but maybe we should attempt to understand it. The media will not explain. You and I must settle on the understanding that no matter what the mainstream may claim, "It's just different" for Black people.

Because of the generalization of Black people, other cultures of people including law enforcement agents treat Blacks according to what they have learned about us second hand.

We notice others as they behave like they fear us, clutching their valuables, and frowning while judging us for our cultural expressions.

As for law enforcement, when they see or approach Black people, their racial profile training and the imprinting that the media in America has crafted about us creates a tension filled and sensitive event more times than not.

I am not the first person to present these observations; this stuff is common knowledge to many scholars and lay people alike.

But I want to help focus our attention on the fact that our cultural interactions with each other become much more damaging to us when race/culture relations blend with the way America's dominant culture does business. Many times, the biased behavior that began in a cultural or social context is exercised at work by our public servants. Each time this happens it creates an event and environment of inequality.

Throughout history, people have waged war, peacefully marched in protest, filed suit, and a host of other creative actions. Still, Black people are targeted and treated as dangerous criminals based primarily on our appearance and skin color.

Take for example, the shooting of 17-year-old Trayvon Martin by 28-Year-old George Zimmerman "event".

Trayvon who was traveling alone by foot on February 26th, 2012 in Sanford, Florida and paid with his young life for doing nothing other than looking suspicious to a non-Black person who was acting as law enforcement.

This tragic story is just another heart aching example that young Black people (especially young males) are perceived to be a potentially dangerous group and less than human.

On that day, Zimmerman, who claimed to be authorized as a Neighborhood Watch attendant and NOT an official state law enforcement agent, saw a potential "threat" to his gated community.

Against the instructions of a 911 operator whom he was speaking with on his cell phone at the time, he subsequently approached the hoodie wearing, Skittle candy packing 17-year old Trayvon Martin. Then, like we have all witnessed in America over and over again, Zimmerman took Trayvon's life that day with deadly force and was allowed by the responding police officers to go home and sleep in his bed that night.

The question is: *"If Trayvon was a Caucasian or European male, would Zimmerman have ignored him and head on back home? Or would a White kid have suffered the same fate as Trayvon?"*

We can only guess at the answer to this question.

What's your guess?

The Black community stood with outrage "again" and organized as we have proven we will do, but no amount of (Hoodie) "Demonstrations", monetary compensation, or the incarceration of Zimmerman will bring back his life – Trayvon Martin is DEAD and NOTHING will bring him back.

While awaiting trial, George's brother, Robert Zimmerman Jr., has been granted mass media coverage appearing on several news networks including CNN in an effort to protect his family name and to explain to the public that his brothers story of self-defence is true (as if he could possibly know that). The well-spoken and well coached Robert Zimmerman politely makes the case that the story told by the 911 audio "recording" of George Zimmerman and the 911 operator which holds irrefutable evidence of George chasing Trayvon is fantasy or myth.

Sure, Robert Zimmerman has a right to speak out on the behalf of his family, I agree with that, but how and why are some many major networks granting the Zimmermans a chance to sway the public's opinion by using the media to hold court?

Robert Zimmerman was not at the scene of the crime and any words about the case from his lips cannot be more the mere hearsay and a game of jury pool manipulation. The public has reportedly supported George Zimmerman with tens of thousands of dollars in donation towards his legal costs and the mainstream media has given him a stage to speak to the public.

Alan Morton Dershowitz who is a long time Harvard Law School professor and high profile criminal appellate attorney gave his opinion on Fox news about the way that the prosecution has mishandled the case. He opined that George Zimmerman will be acquitted for lack of evidence amongst other things, which would likely result in more riots from the Black community.

When this tragedy first hit the news, I recall reports that there was a drug and background check executed on Trayvon Martin as he lay dead, but the gunman, George Zimmerman, was not tested?

It seems to me that many people are working in concert to justify the murderous actions of George Zimmerman.

Seating with that for a moment as I attempt to keep writing. It breaks my heart to know that our children do not know racism like we do but they are sure to learn like this child did as he died alone at the hands of 28-year old Zimmerman.

Individually, we each should take on the responsibility of arming our children and ourselves with knowledge about the place we live, in an effort to prevent a repeat of these tragic events like Trayvon's story or other of slain young Black men such as Oscar Grant who also lost his life, at the hands of so-called authorities.

Oakland California's Bart Police Officer Johannes Mehserle (who just so happens to be a White man) murdered Oscar Grant execution style by shooting him in the head on New Year's day of 2009. Mehserle was sentenced to two years in prison and was released from prison on or about June 13, 2011.

Yet some people will argue that racial profiling doesn't exist and that the criminal justice system is fair and just. They will argue this even though the statistics reported by the United States government annually tells a story of nationwide attack on Black men and their families.

Imagine the thoughts and emotions that overtake the Grant family every New Year's Eve. Reminded of this country's violent history as the people around them in Oakland, California celebrate the beginning of a new year with explosions and gunshots, knowing that Oscar's murderer is celebrating life somewhere.

I am sure that the families of the many young men and women who lost their lives before their time would agree that as we collectively struggle for representation we must individually represent ourselves on a case by case basis. I contend that in order to do that, we must have historical perspective, an education and a keen strategy that will help us in our path to self-preservation in America.

CHAPTER 6 - STAYING BLACK

FREEDOM IS NEVER GIVEN; IT'S WON. - PHILIP RANDOLPH

It's how to overcome these conditions that we obviously haven't figured out yet. And it's unlikely that one book can solve all of our troubles. But we can chip away at a part of the problem right now.

Let's start with this:

What exactly do we mean when we say "We must overcome?"

I suppose we are talking about a particular set of conditions:

Condition 1 - Miseducated;

Condition 2 - Mistreatment to the level of social degradation;

Condition 3 - Misdiagnosis and doping;

Condition 4 - Manipulated when Driving While Black:

This set of conditions is a crisis of the mind that nobody, other than those who live the Black experience, is burdened with aiding unless they volunteer to.

MIS-EDUCATION

PROBLEM: The rules that people have used for thousands of years to interact with each other in a civil society is the road map. It guides what we should do with our lives and how to do it so as not to crash up against another person and their right to live their lives. It's been told that we are the people lost in plain sight because we are confused about how to coexist in harmony with others in this world. This causes us all a great amount of continuous stress when any amount of conflict arises in or lives because we aren't sure of the best way to resolve it.

GOAL: The ability to meet our challenges on our path to pursuing our goals without being dependent on others.

SOLUTION: To identify a short list of bodies of knowledge that will allow us to be the most independently capable of dealing with the normal happenings of life. We must become capable of generating enough value with our energy to trade for sustainable income that wills our families and us to grow financially. We must know how to manage risk and that includes the ability to effectively question those who oppose us in a clever and systematic way.

LEGAL MAXIM: THE LAWS SERVE THE VIGILANT, NOT THOSE WHO SLEEP.

MISTREATMENT - SOCIAL DEGRADATION

PROBLEM: Institutional racism has way of caging its victim into feeling trapped by his or her own inadequacies. The continuous attacks on Black people and their way of life weighs heavy on the minds of a Black person when they are attempting to achieve even the smallest of goals. The badgering that we experience is almost invisible to those who do not live our experience. The pressure is enough to imprison a person in their own insecurities and leaving them never to attempt to break the constraints of the opinions of others.

GOAL: To accept who you're and always maintain an understanding of self-worth. No matter your level of education, net worth, or any other status level.

SOLUTION: Surround your environment with people and things that remind you of your self-worth. Make a habit of keeping close relationships with people who appreciate you for who you're and not only for what you can help them with, money or otherwise.

LEGAL MAXIM: WHAT IS NOT VALID IN THE BEGINNING DOES NOT BECOME VALID BY TIME.

MISDIAGNOSIS - DRUGS

PROBLEM: Drugs have been used in our communities as a band-aid for so many of our deficiencies. Schools introduce them to us very often without any proper testing. Grown-ups often sell them to supplement their economic needs in addition to taking them to escape the pains of their reality. The problem with this is that drugs usually cause people more long-term trouble than the short-term fix is worth.

GOAL: To have the ability to face our realities and embrace them with a sound mind. Allowing us to enjoy our relationships and/or our bodies without abusing either.

SOLUTION: Recognize the effects of drugs on those around you and use that analysis as motivation to steer clear of drugs. Instead, work on yourself to build the skills needed to manage your own mind and your body to meet whatever standard of life you choose.

LEGAL MAXIM: THE OLD WAY IS THE SAFE WAY.

MANIPULATION - DRIVING WHILE BLACK

Anyone who has been through the types of exchanges with the police as I have will tell you to approach any encounter with law enforcement full of concern, caution, and a competent understanding of all of the elements of that particular encounter.

A high level of discretion is a must because of the large number of Black families throughout the history of the United States which have been physically assaulted, mentally injured, and monetarily damaged by one or several law enforcement encounters that we experience annually.

Driving While Black is the number one way that an abusive law enforcement agent can bully his or her way into a person's life using nothing more than "tricks of the trade", to say the least.

LEGAL MAXIM: AN INJURY IS NOT DONE TO ONE CONSENTING TO IT.

Think about it and imagine how many times a simple Traffic Stop (Terry Stop) somehow turned into a felony stop in the Black community vs. in the White suburbs?

From the many discussions I have had, I learned that many Black people aren't even bothered about getting a ticket or citation. The main concern for a lot of Black drivers is the thought of being harassed, or illegally searched in addition to being interrogated by the overreaching law enforcement officer.

Where are you going?
Where are you coming from?
Where have you been?
Have you been smoking pot?
Have you been drinking?
Is there anything (and by anything, they mean drugs or weapons) in the car that I should know about – blah blah blah?"

This is an example of second-class citizenship, which only affords individuals minimal rights. The ordained Constitution of 1778 guarantees United States citizens certain protections. Unfortunately, these protections do not operate automatically for Black people in this country, and very seldom do those protections operate outside of brave **assertion** on the part of the driver and only in a judicial hearing in a Court Room.

So when we (Black people) are stopped, we worry ourselves crazy about how a so-called "routine" traffic violation can and usually does spiral out of control to a potential life degrading or life-threatening event. And if, by some miracle, it does not get out of control, we find ourselves surprised and bathing in relief.

I know sometimes I found myself wanting to duck and hide when I see the police, and the times that I thought that I couldn't escape, I began to do a quick mental recall of my property. I checked my inventory in order to ensure that all my credentials and papers were intact just in case they hit the lights on me.

The type of Black man that walks away from these unwanted encounters unharmed is the person who remains emotionally calm while applying some version of a systematic system or strategy.

Today, I study and practice **asserting** certain constitutional protections and due process procedures, especially when some overzealous law enforcement agent is trying to abuse his or her position of authority in order to achieve some unknown selfish benefit at my expense.

This takes patience, intelligence, and poise. To assert ones rights requires a private type of education. Who else would study this or risk themselves in working on a different way to protect Black people from controversial racial profiling other than someone that it effects like you and I?

This means that we have no one to turn to but ourselves for answers.

LEGAL MAXIM: LAW IS THE SAFEST HELMET; UNDER THE SHIELD OF THE LAW NO ONE IS DECEIVED.

I reflect on and review my own ideas about living the Black experience in America

I have had the privilege of witnessing first hand and living with the effects of the different levels of double-dealing that is used by people (and companies) everyday as leverage over others.

I know what it feels like to be treated unkindly, unfairly, and unlawfully on a regular basis, despite what any rules allow or any newspaper article read.

Successful or struggling, as far back as I can remember I have been frustrated with the system, with others, and even with myself for many years about how America treats Black people.

Since before I could drive a car, I have been illegally stopped, illegally searched, illegally detained, and illegally relieved of my private property (including thousands of dollars) too many times to ignore.

Even today, when I come across some dude with a badge, who happens to have clearance and a computer, I know that he can find all of that old monkey business and abuse of power that I was a victim of throughout my years on my record. And he can use those records to further investigate and damage me.

The records associated with me that are public suggest that I have a pattern of butting heads with law enforcement, which is not the case at all. But you (the reader) probably don't even believe me fully so why would some law enforcement agent how is already bias against my kind?

LEGAL MAXIM: AN ACTION IS NOT GIVEN TO ONE WHO IS NOT INJURED.

This did bother me in the past but today it's of no effect on me because I understand its purpose and use. It works to make people feel ashamed, embarrassed, and indebted but I no longer feel that way when someone brings up any record of mine.

Because today, I am fortunate enough to have a better understanding. Everything that life has to offer is more achievable to me because of the perspective I have gained about being Black in this country today.

LEGAL MAXIM: THE BURDEN OF PROOF LIES ON THE PLAINTIFF.

I admit that I made my fair share of bad deals. I admit that I didn't always use my advantages and skills or my business momentum effectively.

However, that doesn't mean I was naïve; it means I was learning what I had not been given the chance to learn in public school. I had to learn to deal with the setbacks just like anyone else who was raised in the parts of the city where the people are socially and economically broke.

I recognized that people other than Blacks do also deal with these same realities, especially those people who are familiar with living with the effects of being surrounded by a community of people who are living below the poverty line.

I think that the only difference is that the odds of overcoming the pitfalls of poverty is widely different and favor non-Blacks, of course.

As the "mis" educated people, many of us have a habit of expressing our emotions as a method of communicating our dislike or contempt, yelling, and swelling up attempting to gain control.

But in today's world, this method may work in very few settings but on a business level or in a public arena, it will only make you look foolish or insane.

Maybe others have it easier and maybe they don't but either way, I found that when I started to accept who I was relative to the places I go, I began to have more satisfying results in my business and my social life. It dawned on me one day, something just clicked in my mind, and I became more deliberate in my approach to living in this world as a Black man.

As the saying goes, "if you work hard in America, you can get ahead."

Not for Black people. For Black people, we must read between the lines and work smart in addition to working hard; otherwise, we will just be spinning our wheels.

My ticket out of those dark trenches of ignorance wasn't fixing my victim's complex and negative attitude, although that was a part of it. I also learned to approach all of my setbacks in a systematic way instead of approaching them while I was emotionally out of balance.

I could see clearly that racism was affecting us all in many ways, but it could be handled with style and skill if I could just keep my cool long enough to weigh the facts.

Black people can never expect to receive any courtesies. We must always know the rules and be prepared to govern ourselves to the letter of the law in addition to having the courage to hold others accountable.

LEGAL MAXIM: THE CUSTODY OF THE LAW IS STRONGER THAN THAT OF MAN.

Practicing putting things into a Black experience as a context will help us take the appropriate action rather than resorting to violence and irrational means that may fulfill an urge but is only counterproductive to the reaching of your desired and particular goal.

Some people will say:

"Yeah, I know but sometimes I just can't help it - and I go off."

This is because it's one of the only few ways that we know how to possibly gain control when challenged.

This is our response by design of cause and effect. Others have deemed us Blacks as the people with fewer rights than others. The facts suggest that other people target us and when we attempt to overcome or meet conflict, we find ourselves handicapped by a handcuffing second-class education that we received from our schooling.

Often, after we exhaust ourselves trying to force our way through the conflict, and left with frustration with nowhere else to turn, we begin to misplace our spiritual means of problem solving and try to address our physical world's problems with prayer.

Prayer and faith have their place and Black people should use them in a way that is private and personal as opposed to calling on faith when conducting business.

LEGAL MAXIM: SUNDAY IS NOT A DAY IN LAW.

Regardless of how we style our approach with the use of religion or prayer, we cannot afford to have our spirituality make us passive about our business affairs.

Prayer, morality, and psychological efforts are used in social interaction as tools of motivation.

How should you compel someone to stop physically abusing you?

Not with prayer - I say.

Hell no — I don't subscribe to that method.

Common sense tells me that praying for someone to physically stop abusing you is an insane idea.

I am not suggesting that you use some unjust means to protect yourself, but do not be surprised when your misguided plea in your prayers goes unrecognized.

LEGAL MAXIM: A WRONG DOES NOT EXCUSE A WRONG.

On the same note, who would even suggest that you should be so passive as to allow someone else to abuse your body and inflict harm upon you or your property? Why must you accept this?

What is the reasoning behind this logic?

As Black women or Black men, we must thrive to be businesswomen and businessmen. Because like or not, others will attempt to force their business on us nonstop, and we must respond in a culturally acceptable manner if we want to have a chance at winning here.

LEGAL MAXIM: LEGAL FORM IS ESSENTIAL FORM.

You and I have been misled from the things we need to know or understand to be high achieving businessmen and businesswomen, or creative people in general.

We have never been taught to **think critically** about anything of significance to our economic welfare.

I have had to find this understanding for myself, subsequent to having great successes at a young age and great failures economically as well. I wanted to know why I had fallen from success.

LEGAL MAXIM: IT'S A FRAUD TO CONCEAL A FRAUD.

I wanted to know what were my disadvantages and weaknesses. I had trouble finding any other person to advise me, who could give me a complete explanation that I could measure and use to make adjustments with.

I asked myself the question: If I did have a private, self-initiated and sophisticated type of education than what commercial, industrial, and professional skills would I have learned with this education? Or what would I want to have gained from it?

This hypothetical situation leads me to discover the kind of tools and abilities that I needed or was lacking for myself.

I discover through self-evaluation that if I had a more sophisticated education, I would want to gain the "means" to question those who oppose me and the ability to meet life's professional challenges systematically and with vigor.

The "means" for a Black man today equals equal-access to capital and the access to the type education that will prepare us to manage that capital.

I believe that if we had the "means", then we could build wealth while avoiding many of the setbacks that those of us with a practical education endure from the stifling conditions that come standard for a Black man and his family in this world.

All of us - Black women and men need a systematic approach to Driving While Black and living life Black in America. That is, if we intend to "Stay Black" and drive.

CHAPTER 7 – THE STATUS OF THINGS

NO MAN MAY MAKE ANOTHER FREE.
- ZORA NEALE HURSTON

Robert L. Wilkins won a civil damages' case against the state of Maryland. In doing so, he shed light on the widely known and common practice used by law enforcements which is the targeting of Black men driving late model vehicles. In 1992, Wilkins, a lawyer at the time (and eventually he became a Judge) was racially profiled and stopped by a cop. When compelled to give an explanation on the record of why he stopped Mr. Wilkins's vehicle, the cop purported to only be acting on the instructions of the superior officer's command. That command was to target Black males in expensive cars. We owe the popularity of the term **Driving While Black** to this case.

This supports the position that Black people aren't appreciated in this country. But everyone always seems to appreciate the movement of money regardless of who is moving it (you can always count of the greed of mankind).

Is it just me or does it seem that Black people are taken more seriously in the professional world when some money is on the line, like the state of Maryland's money that was awarded to Mr. Wilkins and his family?

Working as a district attorney in the 1990's and, eventually, becoming a judge, it's obvious that this particular Black man had some political influence.

Shortly before Rodney King's 1993 victorious effort in civil court on April 29, 1992, the jury acquitted three of the policemen who viciously attacked this man on camera. Rodney King won a civil damages' case against the state of California for 3.8 million dollars close to 2 years after his famed Terry Stop in which he was beaten to within inches of his life.

The acquittals in the case sent the Black community into a frenzy, birthing the worst riots in California history. The damage to the city from the riots reportedly cost more than $1 billion dollars in damages and sparked mini similar riots across the nation.

It's commonly known that Rodney King had no political influence worth mentioning. However, the case was so highly profiled in the media that an attorney's career could benefit financially from handling this case, and handling it well. We need to understand what truly motivates an officer of the court to do as they should.

One thing about the Rodney King case that is rarely discussed anymore is that; if a stranger had not used a personal video camera to video record Rodney King being beating by at least four officers, then the LAPD would have "followed procedure" and made sure that the Rodney King story was never heard.

LAW SCHOOL

Admittedly, law schools create lawyers and "colleagues" of lawyers out of diverse people. And, yes, these colleagues do each other favors. Judges and lawyers share an exclusive code of ethics they sometimes refer to as "professional courtesy", similar to a fraternities secrets and such. They need not know a brother (or sister) to extend them this treatment, but only that they have had a similar experience or trained belief system that they learned in law school.

Consequently, judges and opposing counsel may scrupulously make an attempt to block their (wronged) colleague's right to a legal remedy as they might a non Bar Card carrying pro se litigant.

Q: Can you do as Robert L. Wilkins did, sue and win?

A: Hell Yeah - you can!

Q: Is it a formidable task?

A: You better know it's.

However, although it may be difficult to pursue your claim in civil court:

- If you have taken the steps to create a recording of the event(s);

- Established that the offender does have a duty to uphold;

- That said duty was breached in a way that damaged you and;

- If you can properly present this type of case in court;

Then, no matter if you have colleagues in that venue or not, the odds are on your side that you will be made whole again.

This type of preparation doesn't just happen by accident. If you want to be able to stand up for yourself and assert your own interest effectively, then this is the only way. First, we must all start by adopting some business and legal principles that most of us have yet to confidently operate well on day-to-day basis. This type of effort and educated plan-of-action is missing from most of our academic toolboxes.

All it takes to implement that type of systematic approach is a routine that begins with a reoccurring review of the work that is at hand. It's being proven, time and time again, that to sustain any kind of success takes repetition. You know the saying, "practice makes perfect."

A systematic approach is what it takes to deal with a "Terry Stop" because so many decisions must be made and made fast. But more importantly than that is our ability to see Driving While Black in the context of just another type of goal that we choose to have. How do you pursue your goals? How do you prepare for the journey or the job?

Individually, our wants, needs, and our goals will change and change often. That is a natural part of life. So to prepare for our rapidly changing wants, we must have a way of pursuing our goals that is effective, efficient, and flexible enough so that when our goals change we can switch our attention and reappoint our resources towards our new goal - get it?

All good businessmen and businesswomen are able to make good decisions because they have built the thinking muscle by exercising a process of critical thinking. And they can unleash that muscle on anything that wants to move.

There is a valuable mental review that should become habit for all Black men and women as they are conducting their business of life in America.

And it should be used to help make good decisions in tough times.

It's normal for anyone to become emotionally upset from time to time. It's just human nature. So when this happens and a person becomes upset or confused about a business decision or a personal relationship decision,

I suggest that he or she use what I call the **FOUR FUNDAMENTALS OF CRITICAL THINKING** to help them find calmness again.

Asking yourself these questions puts you back in control and helps eliminate the confusion that might be causing you stress.

FOUR FUNDAMENTALS OF CRITICAL THINKING:

- Sound Reasoning

- Self-Initiated (and Sophisticated) Education

- Social Resourcefulness

- Self-Reliance

Example of reviewing yourself

- What is your state of mind (are you calm enough to reason)?
- Who educated you about what you intend to do (are you sure of your correctness)?
- How are you measuring/leveraging your resources (what will it cost to go forward with your goal)?
- Are you currently being self-reliant (whose advice are you using and why)?

For Black men and their families, critical thinking is the one thing that will either provide the ability to cultivate fruitful lives or the lack of ability to do so.

Our opinions of success will often vary but the path to it looks very similar ever time.

Below is my insight to each phase of critical thinking for and about anything.

Sound Reasoning

Until ones business and life experience lends her the poise and perspective needed to remain calm, goal driving and operating within society with honor, one should research and adopt **Legal Principles (Maxims)** as a way of measuring what the right or wrong thing to do is. Maxims are considered to be self-evident and have no need to be debated by man.

Often the price you may have to pay to pursue your interest versus the worth of that achievement just isn't worth the risk.

Use **Legal Principles (Maxims)** to guide and govern your actions and decision making, in all your business affairs. Maxims help you take the guesswork out of knowing what is considered so-called fair or unfair.

If you're not a benefactor of successful and profitable nepotism, which gives a Man or Woman a private education from a person(s) with a true vested interest in their success, then you may want to consider adopting the **Legal Principles (Maxims)** to apply to your daily operations and conduct. They will help you be in alignment with all doctrines associated with business and legal affairs.

www.uslegal.com presents the definition of Maxims as:

Maxims are a general principles of law embodied in familiar phrases which are used as guiding truths by both judges and lawyers. They are listed in the codified statutes of most states, and are used to determine the equity of a situation.

Self-initiated Sophisticated Education

It's common for a person to be educated by an institution of some kind only to depart that particular program (college or trade) with little more ability to make the entire pieces and parts of their tutelage work together well enough to actually make a career.

We are in no way born with the ability to discern what we should focus our learning on. And because there are bodies of knowledge that have not been emphasized well enough in today's modern society, we can only count on someone with intrinsic motivation to help us determine what's best to learn. But what if your loved one is wrong or cannot help you in this area? Then, you should take my and advice and remember this:

No matter what you have done or will do in the future, the majority of your interaction with people in any capacity is affected by contracts. You cannot afford not to study the principals of contracting - early and often.

This is one education that every man should give himself. An education and ongoing study of the substantive civil law category called Contracts.

If you do not choose to learn principles of contracting on your own, you will most surely be taught the hard way by the economy that you subscribe to and/or work in.

I implore you to become what I call a "Contract Scholar"

This particular doctrine is known to be easy to comprehend because it's written in our nature, meaning that many of the principles we naturally subscribe to. I am fully aware of my deficit in this area of my understanding and education with respect to contracts. Are you aware of yours?

Social Resourcefulness

Use your resources to do what makes you healthy and happy first. Life can only be continued or developed by the leveraging of money and managing the exchange of value between you and others.

The **FOUR FUNDAMENTALS OF CRITICAL THINKING** help you apply the good decision making about how to invest your precious resources of Time, Money, Energy, and the Resources in control of those you have good rapport and influence with. Business is not always just business. Sometimes you have to use your reach and personal relationships to help you reach your business goals. Feelings change like nothing else. Be sure to review your goals often and ask yourself what makes you feel good and is good for you. This is the most important place to focus your valuable resources.

Self-Reliance

You will eventually learn (or as I like to say) "re-learn" that the Law does allow for self-help in legal matters and likewise in business affairs, but only within reason as society frowns on overreaching.

Society appreciates legal process that steers clear of vigilante type of behavior, or unjust retribution. Becoming self-reliant and learning to be totally responsible for your ability, or lack thereof, to meet your challenges without depending on anyone else is the most control any of us will ever know.

Who is in control of your life?

Do you stand by and watch while someone else manages your affairs, like the cop standing at your window who is rushing you to agree with "his" business?

Now that we have an idea of whom to think about business, let's look at what to do in business.

All business affairs boil down to these 7-steps every single time.

It's important to understand that language and the meaning of words can make it very difficult to comprehend what is happening for you or against you in business.

So I recommend that you get a grasp of legal terms because they will affect you all your life.

Slang, and even the common meaning of words, that you and I use in everyday speak will change in our lifetime but the definition of legal terms aren't likely to change in our lifespan.

The courtrooms and officers of the court including police officers across the nation will use legal terms against you if you let them. Therefore, I suggest that you look up these words below in a Black's law dictionary, and continue the practice using this type of legal dictionary throughout your life in business.

THE 7-STEPS TO ANY TRANSACTION REVIEW:

- Offer (The act of presenting something for acceptance)

- Acceptance (A buyer's assent that the goods are to be taken in trade)

- Surety (Collateral, liable for the payment of another's debt)

- Record (Written, contract, evidence of an event, documents, etc.)

- Accounting (Version, story, history, delineation, etc.)

- Performance (An obligation that is due under contract)

- Enforcement (The act or process of compelling compliance)

Here is what a 7-step review might look like when conducting business. Ask yourself these questions:

- Offer: Are all the terms of the particular offer being made clear?

- Acceptance: Is there any evidence that the offer has been accepted?

- Surety: What is pledged in case the parties fail to perform?

- Record: Do I have a contract or record of the binding agreement?

- Accounting: How will the accounting records be kept for accuracy?

- Performance: What is each party obligated to do or NOT do?

- Enforcement: What is the lawful and reasonable enforcement option if either party fails to perform?

This routine review (above) will apply to any transaction that you might be a party to.

Remember, all business uses transactions big or small to function and facilitate all trade between the business and its customers or other businesses alike. So you always know what is going on with your business affairs if you know these 7-steps.

Trading valuable products and services between Party A and Party B is usually where we win or lose. We have to make better decisions in this area.

This process is economic in purpose and it applies to absolutely all business including traffic citations. Every step of a transaction is important, and there are many complexities to learn about the way each of them can possibly be used.

However, there is one part of a transaction that is the most important in regard to establishing leverage in that area of your business. Creating the type of record or **contract** that favors you and your interest is the most important thing you can do when conducting business.

Because no matter what happens in that transaction, if there is every any question or dispute, the law of that particular deal will start with the letter of that **record** or **contract**. So if that record reads in your favor, you will have the best chance of being profitable one way or another.

When you find yourself in conflict in business, these are the 7 questions (above) and concerns that will help you sort them out. Offer and Acceptance are most commonly coined as a 'meeting of the minds'. If you have ever been pulled over, you know that it does not feel like an offer when the police start talking, BUT it's.

If you have ever asked an officer if you "must" sign the ticket that he's sliding in your window, the customary response is a "counter offer" from that officer.

To which he would probably say, "If you don't sign it, I have to take you to jail". Now, this is not exactly the truth and, most times, is a bluff. Whether he will take you to jail or not is something we must cover later. The point that I am making here is that it's optional for you to sign the ticket because he said the word "if".

This is just another example that the 7-Step process is always operating when you're interacting with others.

You and I would be far better business men and women if we had been introduced to, and schooled about, this 7-step process and how to operate it as a child and continuously throughout our adult lives.

As long as we live, we will use this process to operate transaction in our social lives, with family and friends, in business with bankers or bread makers. And, yes, you guessed it, even in a traffic stop situation. To explore further the mechanics of transactions, I suggest:

(This is a book title) Brian Blum's on Contracts Examples & Explanations.

Before you find yourself in a **Driving While Black** situation, I implore you to use a routine review similar to the:

- FOUR FUNDAMENTALS OF CRITICAL THINKING and

- THE 7-STEPS TO ANY TRANSACTION processes instead of sitting in anger and frustration.

Become unstuck and move towards your goals without unnecessary delay by using these two simple routine reviews.

The power of progress is vital to us all. The paralysis of analysis is fatal. To keep going in life is the paramount goal. So how can you keep going under a circumstance that Driving While Black might deal you today and still remain calm and clearheaded?

LEGAL MAXIM: ANGER IS BRIEF INSANITY.

By using your routine reviews – that's how.

The typical types of things that we can no longer afford to allow to interfere with our self-preservation are:

- Hecklers and triggers

People say and do things that may cause you to extend or risk your resources by doing things that are counterproductive to your individual interest. Do not fall into this trap of putting other people's agenda on your daily calendar.

- Wage Working

Wage slavery better describes a situation where a person's ability to meet his/her every need depends on the wages received from another, especially from full-time employment. The analogy between slavery and wage labor includes the lack of job choices in a certain economy and lends light to the relationship that an employer has with an employee, and how similar that relationship is to a slave and the Slave Master.

The way to escape from such a hierarchical social environment, and the many threats that are present in this system, is to become an Entrepreneur. To be a creator and express creativity in business and in life. Creativity is rewarded at a far different rate than labor. The self-worth that is displayed through creativity is empowering and needed by all.

- Curricula – Race course

The education you receive from someone else is preparing you to do something. Whenever you're learning, you must consider what the substance of their tutelage is, and why you're studying the particular curricula.

Studying things without clear interest and understanding is spoiling our lives. There is little evidence that a college degree is a deciding factor in a person's chances of reaching their true financial goals. Be more careful with whom you place your trust.

- Crisis and Paranoia

Paranoia is known to consume a person's thought process when that person is heavily concerned by the potential loss of something they hold dear. Any and all perceived threats drive a person to spend energy and valuable resources on far reaching assumptions and conspiracy theories on which the person can blame failures and shortcomings. In most instances, the stress of the competitive lives we lead causes us to have a delusional state of mind. This state of mind tends to accept the persecutory ideas about the environment it's in, and causes the hope-lessness attitude to consume its natural, vibrant, and creative productiveness.

- Summary processes

Many times corporations use administrative processes against us to secure sum-mary adjudication. This means they earn the right to the possession of the property in question without going to trial: a vehicle repossession, a foreclosure. These are examples of summary processes. These processes are a definite violation of due process, and it's your duty to assert your right when you recognize a summary process being formed.

LEGAL MAXIM: IT'S THE DUTY OF A GOOD JUDGE TO PREVENT LITIGATION.

- Challenge and opportunity

Challenge and opportunity alike can be just as harmful to a person's productivity. Either of these will distract you from your path, and usually cause you to waste resources working on things that aren't a part of your preconceived strategy. They should not be allowed to set you back in anyway.

As you may have learned, the "International Monetary System" is the name of the game that we are playing. In order to win any game, the players must be relatively educated about the rules associated with that game. Playing the game is almost impossible to avoid because once you have a birth certificate or social security number you're signed up to play. The winners in the game achieve those results by using every element of contracts and/or law. The small print of a contract is a part of a contract; don't let anything slide when the stakes are high. Educating yourself in the area is the fastest way to manage your financial fears. This is the most beneficial single body of knowledge that anyone can choose not to learn. If you choose NOT to learn this, you're also choosing to remain a certain kind of slave in this world we know today.

One of the most important lessons I learned during my entrepreneurial career is that the advice of others can make or break the entrepreneurial spirit of a man or a woman. The issue is that we are all subjected to bad advice that we purchase from lawyers and other so-called experts. Then, our lives are damaged by the personal interest of that individual who offered such advice, or that individual's personal business mode of operation.

His or her business is only their own business interest and not to your benefit. Your business interest is always yours and not to their benefit. Therefore, you must understand, manage, and accept responsibility for ALL the business transactions you execute in trade. You cannot assume that it's another individual's business to see to it that you succeed over them. There is NO such profession that exists today.

This is evident when you analyze any lawyer's business model. Win or lose, a lawyer of any kind will expect, attempt, and pursue being paid for services rendered.

"F**k you, pay me!"

On top of this, the principles of the contract are what we naturally do to develop our personal relationships in a positive direction, if done right.

Every person who intends to win in this game of life must learn (learn, learn, LEARN) and constantly sharpen their knowledge and skills in respect to contracts. Spend some leisure time giving attention to content related to contract principles weekly. We must know what creates an enforceable contract, what the types of contracts are, and what a legal cause of action is at least.

The ability to articulate the obligations of contracts is a skill that can save any person much Time, Money, and Energy. These valuable resources are the things we trade for good times and feelings like vacations and spa treatments, et cetera.

Money helps to determine our quality of life.

Being competent in this area of reading and understanding contracts will give you the ability to make adjustments in any and all relationships. This is the definition of control/freedom of self because it gives you the confidence to meet your challenges, which has the effect of making you feel powerful.

To become competent in contract/law (a Contract Scholar), you must own, review, and keep readily available at least these books:

- Black's Law Dictionary

Black's Law Dictionary has been cited as an authority in many U.S. Supreme Court cases. It was founded by Henry Campbell Black, contributed to by dozens of academic contributors, and revised at least 9 times to date. Because legal language is important in contracts, a Black's Law Dictionary is essential to your toolbox of books. Pay attention to the Maxims usually found.

- Brian Blum's on Contracts Examples & Explanations

Brian Blum's on Contracts Examples & Explanations This book is required reading for most first year law students. Whether the issue you're addressing stresses policy driven approaches or common law or The Uniform Commercial Code (UCC), this book will help you identify the principles of law that are present from formation to breach (tort or trespass) to remedies.

- A UCC-Book of Your Choice

The Uniform Commercial Code (UCC) is a set of suggested laws relating to international and domestic commercial transactions.

- Nolo Guide on Legal Research

Nolo Guide on Legal Research. This book, in its most current form, will teach you how to answer any and all specific legal questions for yourself.

The best way to sharpen your skills and knowledge is to use them. I mean apply them in a matter that you have an interest in the outcome or result. Apply what you know to conduct better and more profitable transactions with honor and respect for others and their right to contract and **due process**. For this, you will earn others' respect and a reputation of a worthy business man or woman

For those of us who plan to continue Driving While Black, remember that we earn money in order to buy stuff and do stuff we enjoy, and not to pay colossal fines, charges or fees that will not add value to our lives in any way.

So we must learn to stop agreeing to these fines and charges without questioning the validity of them. We must always look to learn how to contract better.

Because if you do not question them, they will ask you to consent to releasing your interest in more and more of your property (money, jewelry, drugs, and weapons). They will do so until they have taken all of your valuables other than the right you gave them by agreeing with their request or acquiescing when they proceed unlawfully.

So what is the next step for you and I?

Learn, think, learn, and think again. Challenge yourself by thinking about most of everything you do in life as a business transaction.

Go back to the 7-STEPS TO ANY TRANSACTION frequently. Learn from it, apply it, and teach it to others.

If something seems particularly difficult and complex, go back to the FOUR FUN-DAMENTALS OF CRITICAL THINKING. It will help you do your own thinking and decision-making, instead of allowing someone else to do your thinking or decision-making for you.

These two systematic processes will be the key to not only your survival in a hostile experience but to PROSPER beyond your greatest ambitions. No one can stop you when you think critically and deal with every situation as a business transaction.

CHAPTER 8 - DRIVING WHILE BLACK IS A TECHNOLOGY

MASTERING THE HUMAN TECHNOLOGY OF DRIVING WHILE BLACK

I have identified what I think are the most important four steps to protecting ourself during a traffic stop or a Driving While Black type of event. You will read and recognize that they are four things that Black people do (sometimes subconsciously) consistently to defuse the effects of racism in America already. It's my idea that if we zero in on these effective techniques, modify them as needed and use them more deliberately, our quality of life can continue to improve. Below you will find a summary of the four steps that I have identified as best practice:

1.   STEP ONE *Trust but verify*

We all know that there are good people and there are bad people in this world. Both types of people tend to find employment in various businesses and in various capacities in our society including law enforcement. Nevertheless, we all have to embrace some level of trust for others if we want to enjoy life in a sustainable way. But, to trust another person is an individual choice, no one other than self has the authority to tell you or me whom we must trust.

If you or I decided to trust a person and for "good reason", then we should convey our trust in that person and extend them our consent/cooperation without question.

However, if we cannot find a "good reason" to trust a person then we should convey to that person that we have a certain level of trust for that person but we need to verify (in written disclosure);

- Who they are;
- What their official capacity is and;
- What their contact with us is regarding.

Note:

The Fifth Amendment says that no one shall be "deprived of life, liberty or property without due process of law."

The Fourteenth Amendment, uses the same words, called the Due Process Clause, to describe a legal obligation of all states.

These words have as their central promise an assurance that all levels of American government must operate within the law and provide and disclosure fair procedures.

Further, Police take an oath similar to this:

"On my honor, I will never betray my badge, my integrity, my character, or the public trust. I will always have the courage to hold myself and others accountable for our actions. I will always uphold the constitution my community and the agency I serve."

Therefore, it's already agreed by all that you and I have the right to verify before we trust what we are being told.

2.   STEP TWO *Ask questions*

Although it's not often an easy task, we must "Speak truth to power" and everyone else for that matter. We need never compromise our character, our integrity or our contractual agreements by lying. Liars eventually lose by default in this society so we must learn to ask questions in place of fabricating facts.

A lie cannot live. – Martin Luther King, Jr.

Attempting to cause a person to do something by telling that person that such action is required by law, when it's not required by law, may be a felony.

Reference:

18 USC §242 provides that whoever, under color of any law, statute, ordinance, regulation, or custom, willfully subjects any person in any State, Territory, Commonwealth, Possession, or District to the deprivation of any rights, privileges, or immunities secured or protected by the Constitution or laws of the United States ... shall be fined under this title or imprisoned not more than one year, or both.

18 USC §245 provided that Whoever, whether or not acting under color of law, intimidates or interferes with any person from participating in or enjoying any benefit, service, privilege, program, facility, or activity provided or administered by the United States; [or] applying for or enjoying employment, or any perquisite thereof, by any agency of the United States; shall be fined under this title, or imprisoned not more than one year - or both.

42 USC §1983 provides that every person who, under color of any statute, or-dinance, regulation, custom, or usage, of any State or Territory or the District of Columbia, subjects, or causes to be subjected, any citizen of the United States or other person within the jurisdiction thereof to the deprivation of any rights, privileg-es, or immunities secured by the Constitution and laws, shall be liable to the party injured in an action at law, suit in equity, or other proper proceeding for redress.

> **Legal Maxim:** Good faith is to be preserved

> **Legal Maxim:** He who flees judgment confesses guilt.

> **Legal Maxim:** An oath is indivisible and it's not to be held partly true and partly false

The Sixth Amendment: In all criminal prosecutions, the accused shall enjoy the right to a speedy and public trial, by an impartial jury of the State and district wherein the crime shall have been committed, which district shall have been previously ascer-tained by law, and to be informed of the nature and cause of the accusation; to be confronted with the witnesses against him; to have compulsory process for obtain-ing witnesses in his favor, and to have the Assistance of Counsel for his defense.

Note:

"Assistance of Counsel" may imply but does not mandate the use of an Attorney. *It's so important to read laws carefully.*

3. **STEP THREE** *Record for further review*

Many times good cops are compelled to turn the other cheek when they witness bad cops doing dirty deeds. However, this is not an act that comes easy and with-out a level risk and stress for each officer who chooses to turn the other way when injustice is happening.

Do not underestimate the power of knowing your rights and recording every viola-tion for further review by yourself and others. When any person, law enforcement or not is put in a position where they could possibly become liable for a claim or a charge they begin to behave more carefully and deliberately.

LEGAL MAXIM: ABUNDANT CAUTION DOES NOT HARM

It might even weight on a good cops conscious and cause a division that can work in our favor if the process proceeds.

Also, courts weigh claims, so if you find yourself in a Court room with no evidence of your claim, then you're of no threat to your adversary and have little chance of prevailing.

The Federal Rules of Civil Procedure is far less than 100 pages of (easy) reading and it can help us understand the standards that we need to meet to raise a claim against someone who has violated us.

Let's make no excuses for ourselves, we must make an agreement with ourselves to be prepared to record our Driving While Black events at all times by keeping with us these items:

1.   Recording Devices(s)
2.   Public Servant Questionnaire(s)
3.   Witness Affidavit(s)
4.   Pen and Pad
5.   A copy of the Constitution

4.   STEP FOUR *Patient and persistent*

People will interfere with your progress and growth, with both good and bad intentions. But, if and when the issue at hand is important enough to you then you're entitled and obligated to identify and execute the most effect process that will take you towards your goals.

Sometimes you will need to experiment with a strategy or technique, so don't be afraid to make mistakes. With bold action comes the need to redirect or correct errors. With the fair and just intentions nothing unmanageable can happen from your relentlessness.

Because most people just go with the flow there is a disproportionate number of people that will not want to face the harsh realities that we face daily. For that reason we need to solicit feedback and support from people who will use their own intelligence to help analyze circumstances rather than acting out of fear or another emotion which has the effect of making a person more irrational.

The laws today read in our favor in most cases but it's the enforcement of those laws that eludes us. In order to experience better results here in America has an oppressed people we must first maintain the desire to be freed from our mental bondage.

We must change our approach and with any new skill or goal there will be a learning curve. So we must also realize and accept that we will have to be patient and persistent if we want to affect and realize positive change.

LEGAL MAXIM: FAITH MUST BE GIVEN TO LATER DECISION

CHAPTER 9 – STEP ONE

TRUST BUT VERIFY

Note: I am offering this process with the presupposition that someone is recording the event to the best of their ability using any and all technologies at the disposal of the people party to the event. This includes but is not limited to a pen and pad, recording device and/or a video camera of some kind.

1.   When an emergency vehicle and its company (squad car is an emergency vehicle) are delaying you, the smart thing to do would be to safely secure your car out of the way of traffic or any possible dangers of the immediate environment.

2.   Keep the doors of your vehicle locked and roll down the window half way up (or a little higher). According to the law, you're well within your rights to feel safe and secure. Rolling down your vehicle's window is simply an invite for others to reach in.

3.   Do yourself a gigantic favor, simply tell yourself that regardless of how uncomfortable you may be, the matter is not personal, it's just business.

4.   Gently place both hands on your steering wheel in plain view where the police officer can clearly see them and then wait for the officer to approach you. At this point, DO NOT begin to search for your driver's license, papers, or permits.

5.   Do not interrupt the police office while he or she is speaking; wait until they offer you a chance to respond.

6.   Understand that it's a business transaction when the officer presents the initial offer verbally. So you should not assume anything, simply pay close attention to what is said.

Regardless of what is said, it's ALWAYS an offer to which you have a right to counter ("counter offer") or clarify.

7.   By choosing to answer with a question (see below for examples) to any offer that the police officer makes, you can ESTABLISH by verbal agreement with the officer that there is no rush. Thus, both parties need not make any hasty or irrational decisions. Do not allow the situation to push you into making uninformed and rash decisions in any traffic stop situation you may find yourself in.

Here are some examples of responsible questions you might ask:

- Is there an emergency?

- Is there something that I can help you with today, officer?

- If you're in a hurry, am I free to go?

- May I ask you a few questions before we proceed?

Getting Down to Business

By asking the questions that are listed below in the most polite manner, you will be able to establish an agreement with the officer in regard to the officer's status relative to yours:

May I please see your picture identification, officer?

If the officer presents a state of federal issued identification with a photo on it, then the officer has represented that that he or she is there in the capacity of a citizen. This means that he/she is deposed of official office and grants with no official capacity to act on behalf of the state or entity other than conducting his/her personal business. You do not have a binding agreement with the citizen, but it's assumed that you have an agreement with the state to follow certain traffic codes.

> *Important Note:*
>
> According to the law, police officers in the capacity as "officers" have been authorized to arrest/detain citizens in the capacity as an "individual" for a reasonable amount of time to investigate a particular crime (how much time is "reasonable" time?). However, it's against the law for one citizen to detain another if the other has not committed an offense. So, if the officer produces an ID, he or she has simply made herself no different than an "individual" standing in line at the supermarket. What this means is that the previously supposed authority or duty (as an officer) to detain/arrest anyone is no longer a function of law in that instant matter. This is important to understand because this is what we are working against when we are being pulled over. However, although understanding this is crucial, attempting to explain this to anyone to compel cooperation is ill-advised.

Why You Need to Ask for the Officer's Identification

Doing this helps to allow for "equal" protection under the law (this is a 14th amendment protection). Though there is a possibility that this will not happen; but if it does, you will have all the necessary identification of the officer in order to file a future claim against his/her person aside from their Department or company. This can be quite compelling to any officer, because his or her income can immediately become affected with your claim.

What if the Officer Refuses to Produce Photo Identification?

If the officer refuses to produce photo ID, and insists that you produce your identification, you're duty bound to do the following:

- Carry on by presenting to the agent the form *Public Servant questionnaire* to be completed by you or simply begin to ask any of the following questions;

- "Am I not due equal protections under the law per the 14th Amendment, 1868, Section One (1)?"

- "Do you not have a duty to uphold the Constitutional Protections?"

- "Are you refusing to identify yourself?"

- "Does your request for my License and Registration not constitute a search without a warrant, infringing on my 4th Amendment protections?" Or;

- "Are you not sworn or affirmed to uphold the 5th Amendment – because you're suggesting that you have the authority to deprive me of my property (your name is your property) without just compensation or due process of law?"

  Important Note: You have a civil duty to provide "reasonable" identification AND so does the person who initiated the stop. So, if you provide a writing or a badge of some kind with a name on it then you may have met your duty. You might notice that law enforcement agents provide agency identification and not State ID. This is considered "reasonable" identification and is in accordance with the law.

This is the time where you swoop in and make your offer

The offer you make could be similar to:

I am unsure of your official capacity; so, with all due respect, kindly have your

"Watch Commander" join us, and I will try my best to reach my attorney in case we might need some legal assistance. (The more people present, the better for you because each individual will become a **witness** to any and every trespass on your rights).

Tip 1: Watch commanders and superior officers are often busy with other important administrative tasks. They will not be pleased about being called to a mere traffic stop situation. It's a reasonable "counter offer" to request for the audience of the law enforcement agent's superior officer. This means you're refusing the initial offer and replacing it with a new one which is one that is more suitable to protect your interest.

Tip 2: If the superior officer (or any other agent for that matter) joins the traffic stop "business meeting", you should ensure that you address him/her with the utmost humility and courtesy.

You should also ask them to produce their personal identification.

The offer(s) you have made is now the business to be considered. You can seize the opportunity to negotiate further with a couple of convincing leverage claims. You can also listen to the other party's counter-offer to your (now paramount) offer and make the necessary attempt to settle the matter with integrity.

The other party will be left with just three options:

- Meet the terms of your offer and summon his/her watch commander.

- Turn down your offer and carry on violating his/her oath of office in addition to your unalienable rights (of which you will have a cause of action to sue for damages).

- Politely bring the meeting to an end and part ways.

How to Respond to Options 1 to 3

Responding to Option 1

If, or when, the watch commander arrives – if you want to – you can choose to offer your identity verbally or otherwise as a sign of good fate, then go on to ask the watch commander to investigate the transaction facts by further asking the following questions:

- Has anyone been harmed in the commission of a crime?

- What gives this officer the right to detain me unlawfully for unreasonable amount of time? and/or;

- Am I under arrest or am I free to leave?

- Does anyone here now have the legitimate claim to detain me, i.e. a warrant for my arrest – if so, may I inspect it, please?

Responding to Option 2

Take note of all the parties that you will seek "formal resolutions" jointly and severally to the company they are representing and them individually, but you will not oppose the egregious infringement of your rights under duress, threat and intimidation. Recording the events is the key to raising a claim in the future.

Responding to Option 3

If I am correct, I am free to be on my way, I kindly bid you farewell.

If the adversaries are insistent that you must sign something, anything at all, you should make sure that you ask, "What will happen if I do not sign?" If you aren't satisfied with the answer(s) that the adversaries have provided, you may want to sign the words "Under Duress" right in the signature box. As I mentioned earlier, sign the words LITERALLY! Or in some situations, if you aren't pushed to end the matter forthwith, it makes much sense to refuse to sign anything. In accordance with the law, in many cases, you can go before a Magistrate Judge right away! You have a right to insist on being taken to the magistrate Judge ASAP! – Unless, of course, there is a genuine warrant for your arrest.

Look in the eyes of the officer and calmly ask:

"Is there a bona fide – verified – claim or arrest warrant for my examination – one that I can view this instant?"

Tip 3:

Perception: You need to understand that showing your grasp of the relevant laws while maintaining a respectful disposition will make the other party perceive that you aren't just another "Negro" that they can toy with all willy-nilly. Your air of authority will make them "want" to behave with honor and respect and I suggest you do the same.

What If I Am Asked to Step Out of My Vehicle, What Do I Do Then?

If the officer asks you to step out of your vehicle, you have two options, you could:

- Tell the officer that you feel threatened and you cannot be sure of your personal safety outside the vehicle. Place both your hands on the steering while you say this. Add that you will be more than happy to step out of your car when his superior watch commander arrives. Again, be sure that the window is up high enough and the door is locked because it's common for them to attempt to violently drag you out against your will.

- If you find yourself being compelled to get out of your vehicle, ensure that you secure your vehicle by rolling up all the windows, locking the doors, and then putting the key in your pocket. Doing this will protect your car from being searched by your "implied" consent (emphasis on the word "implied") or otherwise. After you have stepped out of your vehicle, DO NOT allow the officers to violate you or your property by searching or even touching your person without a bona fide – verified – search warrant. Ensure that you say a big fat "NO" to any question that would give them the "go ahead" to search your vehicle.

It's my experience that if we ask the right questions, we will find ourselves being treated with respect and honor in our social lives and in our business affairs.

This method and line of questioning are used to build a record of exactly what happened but also what the intent of each party involved was or is.

Without a record, we have no claim to pursue ever. The main thing that courts do in the name of justice is weigh claims and award damages, and if you have no record then you have no claim, therefore you will lose whether you were damaged or not.

Ask questions that help you build your record, so if you have to, at a later date, you can raise your claim in a Court Room.

BELLO BEY

CHAPTER 10 – SECOND STEP

BE PREPARED TO USE YOUR PUBLIC SERVANT
QUESTIONNAIRE.

The ONLY time that you (an American citizen) should be compelled to utter more than a couple of words to a law enforcement agent is when you're under arrest.

As an American citizen, you have the right to be left alone to enjoy your right to privacy.

Most people call this pleading the fifth.

But what is a little known fact is that you're allowed to request that any law enforcement agent who requires information from you to produce a written disclosure by; THE PRIVACY ACT OF 1974 (Public Law 93-579).

Important note:

You will need to stand your ground on the decision you have made prior to speaking to the official, because they are known to bark threats that may or may not have any merit but regardless of the threats made you have a right to understand the procedure affecting you.

To prepare myself for a Driving While Black event, I carry with me a Public Servant Questionnaire which I can present to law enforcement upon being approached by them.

The Public Servant Questionnaire – What is it?

The Public Servant Questionnaire is a very useful form that helps you in a situation like this to ask some of the most clever questions that you would probably forget to ask otherwise.

Lynn Johnston, the author of Who is Afraid of the IRS, developed this questionnaire. (Libertarian Review Foundation: 1983, ISBN 0-930073-03-7).

The law enforcement agents are required to honor a Public Servant Questionnaire by the Privacy Act of 1974 (Public Law 93-579) as well as Section 552a, Section 552, an amending law to Title 5 and the United States Code.

If you watch the evening news, then you know that there are law enforcement agents who visit honest, law abiding citizens for dishonest reasons. So it's important to know that as a citizen of the United States of America, you aren't compelled by law to entertain the company of a law enforcement agent if you aren't under arrest, I make it a habit to exit encounters with law enforcement agents of which I did not initiate as fast as I possibly can.

When a law enforcement agent visits a citizen, this should be because he/she has an arrest warrant from a judge who has convincing evidence that the citizen was involved in a crime or the agent is cock sure that the citizen is involved in a crime.

You are protected by The Ordained Constitution of the United States of America, 1787's Fifth Amendment not to testify or give evidence against yourself. This Amendment gives you the right to send away (yes, send away) any law enforcement agent or government official who comes to your home or the vehicle without the presentment of a verified bon a fide claim.

But!

This law does not apply when the law enforcement agent comes to arrest the citizen who has committed a crime. So if you're up to no good, you should not expect this amendment to work for you.

On the other hand, the agent MUST have an arrest warrant from a judge who has credible proof that the citizen is responsible for committing a crime.

Okay, what happens when a citizen agrees to help a government agent searching for information?

As a citizen, you might want to courteously tell the government agent that you would only assist the government if the agent is ready and willing to cooperate with you in accordance with the law by answering your Public Servant Questionnaire questions. You will need to do this prior to when the investigative questioning begins.

Remember: You as an American citizen. You have a right to be left alone and to keep your privacy. You have a right to a written disclosure for the reason for the visit.

CHAPTER 11 – THRID STEP

RECORD FOR FURTHER REVIEW

In case your questions are met with stonewalling, one might want to move to step three of the process.

Reminder: I am offering this process with the presupposition that someone is recording the event to the best of their ability using any and all technologies at the disposal of the people party to the event. This includes but is not limited to a pen and pad, recording device and/or a video camera of some kind.

In some cases, a victim of certain Civil Rights violations must resort to reciting and reaffirming a claim of rights. Below I have provided a script that may help you design your own claim of rights to recite if you find yourself being violated.

In order to refute any and all presumptions, notify all parties of your claim of rights by reading the following out loud to all of the parties present:

1. If I am not presently under arrest or under investigation or detention, please return me to my liberties forthwith.

2. I invoke and refuse to waive my Fourth Amendment right to be free from unreasonable searches and seizures.

3. I do not consent to any search or seizure of my person, my vehicle, my papers, or of any property in my possession.

4. Do not ask me about my ownership interest in any property.

5. I do not consent to this contact with you.

Any statement I make, or alleged consent I give, in response to your questions is hereby made under **protest and under duress** and in submission to your claim of lawful authority to force me to provide you with information.

[YOU CAN STOP READING OUT LOUD AT THIS POINT]

When you apply all these steps (found in the last few chapters) together, you will have followed a very strategic process that will help protect you from the damaging effects of Driving While Black.

With the knowledge of this strategy at your disposal, you will feel a lot more confident and independent when you travel on the road, regardless of whether you're transporting products or people or traveling alone.

Don't let fear or panic get in the way of you knowing your rights.

Be brave and be prepared.

CHAPTER 12 - FOURTH STEP

PATIENT AND PERSISTENT

The Fourth Amendment to the U.S. Constitution reads:

The right of the people to be secure in their persons, houses, papers, and effects, against unreasonable searches and seizures, shall not be violated, and no Warrants shall issue, but upon probable cause, supported by Oath or affirmation, and particularly describing the place to be searched, and the persons or things to be seized.

When relying on the Fourth Amendment to the U.S. Constitution for your claim of rights, one should consider that the constitution is a living document and it's, at times, left up to interruption and change.

We must be prepared to argue, litigate or debate our interruption of the law at any moment because many times law enforcement and legal types alike, tend to split hairs about what the law says and/or means. If we plan to use it in our favor, then we must be prepared to articulate it well.

It's a fact that the Supreme Court of the United States has concluded that traffic stops are considered a dangerous situation for law enforcement personnel.

The Supreme Court's conclusion is evidenced by their rulings, such as *Terry v. Ohio*, 392 U.S. 1 (1968), in which the Supreme Court ruled that police may briefly detain a person who they reasonably suspect is involved in criminal activity, the Court also wrote that police may do a limited search of the suspect's outer garments (*and the lung of the vehicle in cases involving vehicles*) if they have a reasonable and articulable suspicion that the person detained may be "armed and dangerous". This procedure is commonly known as a "stop and frisk."

The reason they have concluded this may have something to do with the raw data.

For example, over the past ten years, the data has shown that approximately 5,600 police officers have been the victims of assaults during a routine traffic stop. This number alone is enough to make some officers think twice as they engage drivers in a traffic stop.

On top of that, over 300 officers have been feloniously killed during traffic stops by vehicle occupants over the last ten years. Although this number may seem small compared to the 80,000 officers currently working in law enforcement, it's key to remember these numbers do not include cases of death and assault outside of routine traffic stops.

Many would agree that traffic stops are inherently dangerous and risky (for all) and stands as a significant threat to the physical safety of law enforcement officers. It's not uncommon for routine traffic stops to end violently.

With these statistics in hand, it's understandable that police officers take their own safety seriously. Remember that each officer, although a member of law enforcement personnel, has his or her own family, friends and loved ones. Officers who are lost in the line of duty leave a grieving hole in their families' lives.

Essentially, being prepared to conduct yourself with honor can help prevent many cases of assault and homicide against ALL parties involved in traffic stops. Take the time to learn exactly what the fourth amendment protects and how it relates to people in automobiles in order to reduce confusion and misunderstanding during these routine traffic stops.

Although there are times when it's best for us to stand down at the moment, that doesn't mean that you or I should ever give into injustice.

Frederick Douglass said a speech he delivered back in 1886 that:

"Where justice is denied, where poverty is enforced, where ignorance prevails, and where any one class is made to feel that society is in an organized conspiracy to oppress, rob, and degrade them, neither persons nor property will be safe."

I believe that for this reason we must take a conscious stand for what is right for all people and in a civilized manner.

CHAPTER 13 – THINGS TO RESEARCH

I HAVE LEARNED OVER THE YEARS THAT WHEN
ONE'S MIND IS MADE UP, THIS DIMINISHES
FEAR; KNOWING WHAT MUST BE DONE DOES
AWAY WITH FEAR. – ROSA PARKS

WHAT IS DRIVING WHILE BLACK?

Driving While Black (commonly known as DWB) is a phrase in modern American parlance that refers to the criminalization of Black motorists. There is absolutely no doubt that this trend is powered by racial profiling.

WHAT IS RACIAL PROFILING?

Racial profiling is based on the (erroneous) idea that minorities make up the large number of drug offenders and those who commit violent crime.

The ACLU has argued that pre-textual searches actually "VIOLATE" the key principles of the U.S. 4th Amendment, and cautioned that to authorize such searches was to simply "invite discriminatory enforcement."

However, the court failed to heed the ACLU's warning. Rather, it declared that any traffic offense committed by a motorist was a legal basis for stop, in spite of the officer's subjective state of mind. In order words, the United States Supreme Court's decision has given the police the authority to stop and search any vehicle they want.

[This sounds like the Police can ask you to pull over just because - can this be true?]

Okay, everyone knows that every driver has violated some provision of the vehicle code at some point in their driving life. Still, Black drivers are unduly targeted, stopped, searched, and arrested.

The number of black drivers that get arrested far exceeds that of any other population in the United States. How many times have you watched the news and hoped that the traffic violator who got arrested by the police is not black? I have personally lost count.

Yes, the U.S. government is known to condone and sanction the horrible behavior perpetrated against people of color. It's in your **best interest** to arm yourself with the knowledge to help you navigate the murky waters of Driving While Black.

The founders of this country have written the rules in a style commonly known as the U.S. Constitution. Today, unfortunately none of those individuals who did work together to create clear, socially and morally equal standards to be followed on this land called America are here to see that their desires are carried out and the agreements are kept. The individuals who have become responsible for task of using said Constitution as a guide to maintain public order have become difficult to govern as designed by the founders.

How and why is this the case?

One word - Greed!

By design, the individuals elected and appointed by The People (you and me) to be tasked with said responsibilities are those who hold certain positions in the United States Government/United States Supreme Court. They are to uphold the so-called law (U.S. Constitution) of the land. Unfortunately, these individuals are subject to the money and the powerful influence of groups on special interest groups, corporation. Corporations which are driven by the profit potential to take the financial risk (as opposed to criminal punishment) of doing illegal things in the dark to make a profit or to invest money in influence lawmakers to change the "interpretations" of the law to fit the things that these groups do in the light.

Either way, the individuals named by The People to enforce the law are routinely corrupted by groups and organizations that are currently participating in either modern day slavery or modern day piracy. These groups are willing to exploit any and all people (including their own employees) who aren't shareholders with the same interest as themselves.

WHAT ARE THE DUTIES OF THE POLICE?

1.	Enforce the traffic laws

2.	Respond to criminal reports and activities

3.	Investigate accident scenes

This happens on all levels of law enforcement of any shape or form. The only difference in Federal, State and Local Police is which one of them has the duty to take any of the said three (3) actions in a certain jurisdiction or place.

They are evidence collectors but what they aren't are prosecutors. They aren't judges nor are they the authority over you and me unless we ask them to be.

Misplaced trust is put into the people wearing uniforms in many cases. One of the things motivating officers in many cases is the need to create revenue for their department and employers. This goal totally exploits the innocent misplace trust of the people.

Let's consider what happens when you trust an officer without reason. A Terry Stop occurs and it begins as a civil issue or a business transaction. This is because enforcing traffic laws is considered pursuing a breach of contract if there is a presumption that the "motorist" made an agreement or agrees to be obligated by the statutory laws. This is a so-called contractual agreement between the motorist and the State. The trouble with such an agreement is that it proves to be a one-sided agreement, with a web of civil penalties for victimless crimes. What happens when this trustworthy officer does what they so commonly do by investigating further into you and your affairs against your constitutional protections? What happens when they ask you to step out of the car and consent to a search?

The law allows for certain behaviors from law enforcement but, in most cases, the people sworn to uphold these laws often work around these laws for the purpose of meeting some sort of monetary goal. They do so by their own greed or that of the department of which they an agent for if not for some sort of bias.

WHAT IS THE BIG PICTURE?

First and foremost, you need to understand that the advice of others can actually shape your life in a positive or negative way. The truth is that every single one of us is subjected to the bad advice that we actually get from attorneys and other supposed professionals. Then, our lives become affected because of the personal interest of that person, or the person's business. Remember this: their business is only their business. Your business will always be your business, and ONLY your business. You need to learn to understand, manage, and accept complete responsibility for every single business transaction that you carry out.

So you're either one of these two:

- Transaction Chump – you basically depend on the advice you get from others.

- Not a Transaction Chump – you know and have learned how to manage your business transactions.

Remember: During a Traffic Stop, you should not be intimidated or disillusioned by the appearance of other police vehicles prior to or during your interaction with the officer of the law who asked you to pull over. Just proceed with handling your business accordingly.

WHY THE HELL DOES THE POLICE CALL FOR BACK-UP?

Depending on your geographical location at the time of the Traffic Stop (downtown metro area, the Hood or the Suburbs), the police will call for backup. This is done for precautionary reasons. Believe it or not, the police are as nervous as you are when they jump on your bumper (this is the God-honest truth). Do not even think for a second that they aren't! So, they intimidate you – this is just a ruse to cover up their fears.

These officers only have your license plate details to go on – that is, until they walk over to your car and start bombarding you with questions. After they have asked you (perhaps some of the most ridiculous) questions, only then are they put at ease or even made more nervous than they are putting the officer at ease is something you DO want to do.

WHAT IS THE KEY TO BEING GOOD AT DRIVING WHILE BLACK?

If you are absolutely sure that every single thing is right with your dialogue of words (not regarding your credentials and other effects), then you should be pretty confident in applying the very plausible strategies contained in this book in an effort to achieve your desired result. Despite the reason you're being delayed from your travel, you need to clearly understand that the issue is really not what you think or assume is taking place.

You should not make the mistake of playing the guessing game ask questions for clarity.

DIALOGUE IS THE KEY:

- KNOW the words you speak
- KNOW the law of a "Terry Stop"

The actions between both parties actually determine a favorable outcome for you.

I suggest you do the following when transacting business in a Terry Stop:

1. You MUST listen – in the business community; you must be an "active listener".

2. You MUST be a Contract Scholar – this entails studying every element of the deals that you have made or have the intention of making.

Examples of the deals you made are:

- State issued Identification

- State issued Driver's License

- Government Issued Passports

- State Citizenship

- Vehicle registration

A traffic stop is pretty much the same thing as a car salesman who is offering to sell you a vehicle when you aren't shopping for a one. The only difference is the Police are usually only offering to take your money and give nothing of value in return, if you accept the offer.

But it's ill-advised to become disrespectful or aggressive because this uniformed person does have a few weapons at their disposal and all the back up in the world if you want to make it a physical fight.

Unlike the tactics that you can employ in order to respond to a really pushy car salesman, it makes more sense to use your knowledge of contract principles. This is important while you remain honorable and respectable in a bid to settle the matter when you're on the business end of any and every Terry Stop situation.

Remember: "A traffic stop is a business transaction. The corporate agent (Police) that is contracting with you is interested in completing a concise and profitable transaction quickly and without question, and most importantly "at your expense."

DO I HAVE A CHOICE?

You have control and a voice in what happens to your person and your possessions – and don't you forget it!

You can gain the confidence that you need in order to ease your concerns and worries when you're pulled over, violated, illegally searched, and unlawfully detained. You can easily be prepared to successfully handle any officer of the law who thinks that they can question you about your travels and or your business affairs.

ALWAYS find a way to think about every Traffic Stop in a positive business spirit.

Pointing an accusing finger is the easiest way to shirk the responsibility that you have over your own life. You must understand that YOU and ONLY you have control over yourself, and that facing challenges is just a part of being in control.

When you take FULL responsibility for the feedback that you get from others, you will be able to use a lot more effort to clearly understand the interests of the other party. You become a much better listener, which will make you better when it comes to communicating with others.

With the confidence from the study of my self-imposed curricula, I was able to control the situation by simply asking the officers (and their backup units) the right questions in my latest encounter with a Terry stop. Although I was asked once, I was not forced and did not present my driver's license or proof of auto insurance or registration. After much posturing on the behalf of the agents, I was issued a single ticket, a ticket for expired registration on a vehicle that was not licensed in the state because the sticker on the plate was expired.

Naturally, I refused to sign my name; however, after 45 minutes, I simply signed the ticket with the words "Under Duress" and not a name. I contend that the ticket given to me was issued out of spite and defeat. I knew that there were clear rules to playing this game, so if you know precisely what to say and when to say it. You can avoid opening yourself up to unwarranted liability.

I truly believe that Driving While Black is an event that you can and should prepare for.

Your voice, your mind, and your rights determine what happens to you and your property.

Prepare yourself by sharing what you have read in this book and by practicing your newly adopted strategy with other like-minded people.

CHAPTER 14 – MEET THE CHALLENGE

"YOU DON'T HAVE TO BE A MAN TO FIGHT FOR
FREEDOM. ALL YOU HAVE TO DO IS TO BE AN
INTELLIGENT HUMAN BEING."
- MALCOLM X

We have no choice but to wake up and accept that we can only depend on ourselves in our legal and business affairs.

We need to do what we have to do.

It's essential that we behave a certain way consistently in all of our legal/business affairs.

In the world we live in, this so-called "certain way of behaving" is called "being in honor".

This means to be successful, we need to systematically approach our affairs with business and legal principals and we must honor all of our agreements, we can no longer afford to lie, make excuses, complain or go silent with confusion when conflict arises.

Being in honor is the most important aspect of what we do in our everyday interactions, transactions, relationships, business deals, legal disputes et cetera.   All of our results are directly affected by the words we use to respond in times of adversity.

We have been living under wretched conditions here in America for hundreds of years now, and race is a qualifier for us every day and with everything that we do. But no matter our perceived title or position in commerce, our negotiating skills are what will ultimately drive our individual feeling of success of failure.

We will face many situations in which conflict will arise and challenge will make an appearance once again. Every day we rise, there will be decisions to make and others will judge, charge, accuse, and even damage us.

We will all have setbacks and the threat of loss will present itself almost daily.

We must proceed knowing this to be fact.

But if we are individually prepared for these times, we can feel confident and secure in our own skill set and know how. And that is why we must all decide to learn how to adopt the **FOUR FUNDAMENTALS OF CRITICAL THINKING** review (listed below) as a substitute for an incomplete education, ineffective counsel and/or the unhelpful feedback that we often receive.

FOUR FUNDAMENTALS OF CRITICAL THINKING
To eliminate the spike in emotions, and to find calm clarity, one will use the process

in place of experience.

Routine Review Part 1

- Sound Reasoning is a tool that you will need to be successful on any level worth working towards.

- Sophisticated Education is considered an understanding of yourself and the environment.

- Scalable Resourcefulness is things that you must manage using certain exercises.

- Self-Reliance requires an understanding and it's also an important tool to have in business.

Once calmness is restored to the mind, she or he will use the following process to press forward towards the most beneficial outcome while protecting her or his interest at the same time.

To measure where the risk to lose exists in each step of your business transactions, do this:

THE 7-STEPS TO EVERY TRANSACTION:

Routine Review Part 2

- Offer

- Acceptance

- Record

- Surety

- Account

- Performance

- Enforcement

"This (above) is private due process as we know it"

Each step of your agreements builds on the last. If you overlook or skip your due diligence to risk in any of the 7 parts of a transaction, you're setting the stage for loss of resources associated with that transaction.

Once you have adopted this two-step review process for yourself, you will be ready to effectively exercise your own style of asserting your due process in individual transactions that you undertake in life and business. Without them, you're subject to whatever someone else has in store for you and your precious resources.

It's the operation of due process that will free us from the struggles in our own mind and business. With this adjustment, we will become self-reliant and on a path that will allow us to gain and sustain success.

Once we choose to use this review system, **FOUR FUNDAMENTALS OF CRITICAL THINKING**, we will never feel that we are rendered helpless while our property and investments are stolen, shuffled, transferred, and converted away from our control by the unlawful business models, clever scams and schemes again.

Acquiring the knowledge to meet our challenges without being dependent on some so-called expert has the effect of allowing you and me (us) to take control over our lives again.

Because even when we run our lives obeying every law and respecting every business code, when we put in checks and balance for assurance, we find out that we need that extra help. That we need the **FOUR FUNDAMENTALS OF CRITICAL THINKING.**

Our critical thinking makes us get the most of the consultants, the books we read, and the classes we take. When your mind is both disciplined and knowledgeable, this kind of thinking protects you from the treachery of others. It also protects you from their lies, their ignorance, and their self-serving dealings.

Only then will we be able to see the hypocrisy in our education system, in our legal system, in our politics, banking, government, and law enforcement for what it's. Only then are we in the driver's seat, controlling our destiny on the road and in business.

After looking into the writings and laws that gave birth to all of these systems that are failing, I came to the conclusion that the system does work, just not as promoted. I found that it's the opinion of the jurisprudence that if anyone relies on someone else to handle their affairs, then they deserve what they get. This means that the court looks at anyone with a lawyer (in first seat) as an incompetent and they are treated appropriately. Sounds crazy – right? It's true, see for yourself by looking up:

Corpus Juris Secundum (C.J.S.) legal encyclopedia, volume 7, section 4,

Which says in this pertinent part:

- An attorney's first duty is to the courts and the public; not the client;

- That and a person with an Attorney is a ward of the State and;

- A Ward of the state is an infant or person of unsound mind and placed by the court in the care of a guardian.

I couldn't believe these writings that are found right there in the law library, in the very books that the systems follow to govern its subjects. I thought in that moment that I am somewhat ignorant to how this world really works and I have some reading and writing to do if I want to change that.

I have let others make decisions and instruct me for so long that I forgotten how to make my own informed decisions and take full responsibility for the results I get. I released control, which lead to others taking from me with little difficulty. I forgive myself and accept that my experiences have been necessary for me to build character. I pledge that I will never abandon my duty again. I suggest you do the same for yourself.

Remember this - One of the things that I overlooked was that people of all walks of life (EVERYBODY) often breaks the law and any other rules when it serves their interest to do so. You can count on it.

Because I gathered this newfound (new to me) knowledge and understanding, the feeling of control came to me. I did so also because I began to meet my challenges without relying on others and without just throwing money at the problem like so many of us do.

It's clear to me that preparation equals control – If we prepare ourselves by adopting the **FOUR FUNDAMENTALS OF CRITICAL THINKING** routine review to think about our issues and **THE 7-STEPS TO EVERY TRANSACTION** routine review to guide us in exactly how to execute whatever it's that we might decide to do then our chances of success become greater and more predictable.

It's the time for Black women and men alike to make a transition from hopelessness to a place of self-reliance and control. It's time to accept that being a contract scholar is vital to success.

It's time to accept that being in honor, with due process, makes you King or Queen instead of a chump.

No matter what your situation is, you now have the tools to be calm and make a living regardless of the setbacks you might encounter such as the troubles that come with Driving While Black.

I will leave you with these big picture ideas to consider as you move through this world:

The Problem is : the American culture has always permitted prejudicial policies to excuse the unlawful behavior of some associated with the dominant culture.

The Goal is: not to eliminate prejudice altogether but instead to defuse the effects of prejudicial policies.

The Solution is: to educate ourselves about the doctrines, policies and procedures, and how they were intended to be used vs. how they are being operated, so that we can respond effectively and in our own individual best interest.

If each of us commits to approaching the conflicts we experience such as Driving While Black encounters with style and skill, we will all collectively and individually benefit from a new cultural and new positive social reputation that we will build in the process.

Be Brave – and Be Safe.

Bello Bey

Bello has been able to make the most complex ideas jump off the page and tell wonderful stories of successes that are sure to come. All in an effort to convey his business plans and vision to temperamental hard money lenders and investor types.

Living in Seattle Washington in his young twenties, and in business for himself, Bello learned that he had a unique ability to obsessively (not always in a good away) research and write about certain social, political and legal issues (scandals) that otherwise don't get much run in the mainstream media.

Bello was raised on all things Hip-Hop, and was often in the spot experiencing first-hand the treachery that comes with drug dealing, drug abuse, drug busts and early deaths that happen the hood.

Born Black in America, Bello would tell you that he is obligated to take action to help improve the economic circumstances of Black people. For this reason, he has found himself seriously involved in projects of Black elevation for more than a decade now.

Living in the Bay Area, a place so rich with historical social activism, he has found a more fulfilling topic to obsess over other than trying to raise money from fickle frenemies, while chasing an American dream that he intrinsically rejects.

Bello has been invited onto several media outlets to share his perspective on innovative ways that individuals can use non-traditional approaches to defuse the setbacks that come from America's common practice of economic exploitation and oppression of Black people.

Contact Info:

Twitter:	https://twitter.com/blamebello
Facebook:	https://www.facebook.com/bello.bey
Email:	bellobey@gmail.com

Sources

Decades of Disparity: Drug Arrests & Race in the United States. (2009). Human Rights Watch.

Delores Jones-Brown & Brian A. Maule, Racially Biased Policing: A Review of the Judicial and Legislative Literature, in Race, Ethnicity, and Policing: New and Essential Readings 140 (Stephen K. Rice & Michael D. White eds., 2010)

Emsellem, M. (2005, August). Employment Screening for Criminal Records: Attorney General's Recommendations to Congress. Comments of the National Employment Law Project to the U.S. Attorney General, Office of Legal Policy.

Federal Bureau of Investigations. Uniform Crime Reports.

Harris, P.M. & Keller, K.S. (2005). Ex-Offenders Need Not Apply. Journal of Contemporary Criminal Justice, 21(1), 6-30.

Harris, David A. (1994). Factors for Reasonable Suspicion: When Black and Poor Means Stopped and Frisked. 69 Ind. L.J. 659 Weeden.

Henderson, T.E. (2008). Barriers to Employment & Reentry for Formerly Incarcerated People. Berkley Law. University of California.

Institute on Women & Criminal Justice. (2006). The Punitiveness Report – HARD HIT: The Growth in Imprisonment of Women, 1977 – 2004.

National Center for Statistics and Analysis (NCSA). National Highway Traffic Safety Administration (NHTSA).

U.S. Department of Justice. The DEA Position on Marijuana.

Stop and Frisk Campaign (2013). New York Civil Liberties Union.

Terry v. Ohio, 392 U.S. 1 (1968)

Traffic Stops (2008). Bureau of Justice Statistics.

Whren et al. v. United States, 517 U.S. 806 (1996)

www.ingramcontent.com/pod-product-compliance
Lightning Source LLC
Chambersburg PA
CBHW052135270326
41930CB00012B/2899